AF589169

PRAISE FOR
The Price of Becoming

"I've sat across from countless interviewers—Ryan Hawk makes the rest of them look lazy. *The Price of Becoming* is what happens when someone spends a decade asking better questions than everyone else and writes down the answers. This is the best leadership book of the year. If you want to understand what high performance actually requires, start here."

—Scott Galloway, #1 *New York Times* bestselling author of *Notes on Being a Man*

"*The Price of Becoming* refuses to sell you a shortcut. Instead, Hawk shows how small daily deposits—one hundred shots, five hundred words, a single tough conversation—compound into something that looks like an overnight success to anyone who wasn't paying attention. This is a clear-eyed, powerful book."

—Daniel H. Pink, #1 *New York Times* bestselling author of *Drive* and *The Power of Regret*

"Having led in environments where preparation, discipline, and trust determine outcomes, I found *The Price of Becoming* deeply authentic. Ryan Hawk captures a truth familiar to those in uniform: excellence is earned through consistent effort, accountability, and the willingness to stay uncomfortable long after others stop."

—General Stanley McChrystal (U.S. Army, Ret.), *New York Times* bestselling author of *Team of Teams*

"*The Price of Becoming* is a clear-eyed look at transformation and the cost that comes with it. No hype. No shortcuts. Just the truth about change . . . and the discipline required to sustain it. This is a must-read if you are serious about doing work that matters. Buy it! Read it! Then go forth and CRUSH!"

—Jack Carr (U.S. Navy SEAL, Ret.), #1 *New York Times* bestselling author of *Cry Havoc*

"Excellence isn't a moment; it's a pursuit. It's thousands of small decisions, executed with care. In *The Price of Becoming*, Ryan Hawk shows that greatness is built in the details, in the daily practices that quietly compound over time."

—Will Guidara, *New York Times* bestselling author of *Unreasonable Hospitality*

"Ryan Hawk is a master of dualities: he's a great leader, but he's also a ferocious learner. He's an accomplished athlete, but he has also excelled in the business world. He's eminently interesting, but he's also genuinely interested. Ryan has uncovered the secrets of what the best leaders do and how they think."

—Liz Wiseman, *New York Times* bestselling author of *Rookie Smarts* and *Multipliers*

"I've been on Ryan's podcast twice, and both times his preparation was exceptional. What stood out was that he'd actually thought deeply about the messy parts. That's what this book is about. After interviewing so many elite performers, Ryan has identified the unglamorous, compound practices that lead to sustained excellence. The best leaders know how messy they are. They acknowledge their imperfections. They do the work no one sees. This book shows you exactly what that work looks like and how you can do it too."

—Brent Beshore, founder and CEO of Permanent Equity and bestselling author of *The Messy Marketplace*

"Ryan Hawk is that rare kind of person—a truly curious soul who asks questions that drill down into the heart of the matter, leave space for contemplation, and gently urge his subjects to look inside for answers they might not yet have discovered themselves."

—Robert Kurson, *New York Times* bestselling author of *Shadow Divers*

"I knew Ryan Hawk was serious when he interviewed me. His preparation was exceptional, his curiosity genuine. In combat sports, you see who did the work and who didn't. There's nowhere to hide. Ryan brings that same ruthless clarity to excellence in any arena. *The Price of Becoming* shows exactly what the best do differently. Not the motivational speech version, but the actual daily practices they won't compromise on. If you're serious about your craft, read this book."

—Ariel Helwani, multi-award-winning MMA Journalist of the Year

"Most books about success focus on the highlight reel. Ryan Hawk focuses on the reps—the daily, unglamorous work that compounds into something extraordinary. *The Price of Becoming* is a sharp, practical playbook for anyone willing to stay in the arena long after the excitement fades."

—David Epstein, *New York Times* bestselling author of *Range*

"Ryan Hawk has written a book with a simple, powerful model, and it's filled with story after story from real people who exemplify it. *The Price of Becoming* is not only a practical read, but a fun one."

—Patrick Lencioni, author of *The Five Dysfunctions of a Team* and *The 6 Types of Working Genius*

THE PRICE OF BECOMING

ALSO BY RYAN HAWK

Welcome to Management

The Pursuit of Excellence

The Score That Matters

THE PRICE OF BECOMING

THE COMPOUNDING PRACTICES OF HIGH PERFORMANCE

Ryan Hawk

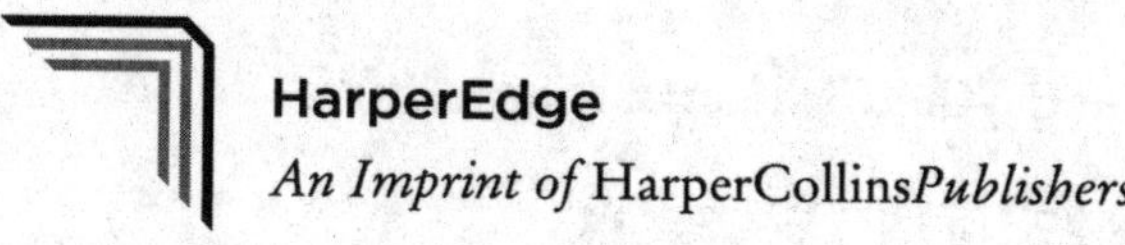

HarperEdge
An Imprint of HarperCollins*Publishers*

 For information, address HarperCollins Publishers, 195 Broadway, New York, NY 10007. In Europe, HarperCollins Publishers, Macken House, 39/40 Mayor Street Upper, Dublin 1, D01 C9W8, Ireland.

HarperCollins books may be purchased for educational, business, or sales promotional use. For information, please email the Special Markets Department at SPsales@harpercollins.com.

hc.com

FIRST EDITION

Designed by Kyle O'Brien

Illustration on p. xviii courtesy of the author.

Library of Congress Cataloging-in-Publication Data has been applied for.

ISBN 978-0-06-348391-0

Printed in the United States of America

26 27 28 29 30 LBC 5 4 3 2 1

*For Miranda, the beautiful**

A self is not something static, tied up in a pretty parcel and handed to the child, finished and complete. A self is always becoming.

—Madeleine L'Engle

Contents

Start Here...xiii

PART I | LEARN

CHAPTER 1
Contemplate, Copy, Create: Building Skills Through Mindful Imitation...3

CHAPTER 2
Curiosity Compounds: Conversation and Exploration...14

CHAPTER 3
Question Everything: Challenging Assumptions for Growth...32

PART II | WORK

CHAPTER 4
The Hard Way: What Everyone Gets Wrong About Strength...57

CHAPTER 5
The Long Game: Daily Inputs,
Extraordinary Outputs...84

CHAPTER 6
Writing and Selling: The "Art" in Articulation...109

PART III | LEAD

CHAPTER 7
Trust Your Wings:
Leading Without Permission...129

CHAPTER 8
Gaining Perspective: Reflection and Intention...153

CHAPTER 9
The Teacher's Path:
Mastery Through Mentorship...173

Keep Going...194

Acknowledgments...201

Notes...205

Index...219

Start Here

At five o'clock on a humid June morning a couple decades ago, my football teammates and I stood sweating on Miami University's practice field when Coach Terry Hoeppner shared what seemed like fortune-cookie wisdom: *"Have a plan, work the plan, and plan for the unexpected."* I nodded along, but it took me years to understand what he was talking about.

I had just moved into a run-down off-campus house with three other players, carrying the kind of bulletproof confidence that only exists in eighteen-year-olds. The plan was simple: become the starting quarterback, win some conference championships, then play in the NFL. Clean and straightforward.

Then reality did what it does best: laughed at my plans.

Another quarterback showed up as part of my freshman recruiting class. After a two-year battle, he beat me out for the starting QB job and would go on to become a first-round pick, win two Super Bowls, and be a future Pro Football Hall of Famer. Me? I learned that plans sometimes fail. But the discipline of planning, thinking through what matters, what could go wrong, what comes next . . . That's what prepared me for a future I couldn't predict.

"Have a plan, work the plan, and plan for the unexpected."

■ ■ ■

I never imagined I'd host one of the most listened-to podcasts or interview some of the world's most influential people. That wasn't anywhere in my original blueprint. But through *The Learning Leader Show*, I've heard it hundreds of times from people like Tony Robbins, Kat Cole, James Clear, and Admiral William McRaven. Their stories all share one thing: none of them went straight up and to the right. They all had detours, setbacks, and pivots that looked like failures at the time.

Life throws curveballs. Plans change. Unexpected events pile up. What separates high performers from everyone else is their willingness and attitude toward working through the uncertainty.

THE PRICE OF BECOMING

It was surreal. I was standing on the hallowed grounds where Colonel Joshua Chamberlain famously ordered his 20th Maine Regiment to charge down the hill with bayonets at the Battle of Little Round Top which led to repelling multiple Confederate attacks. Four-star General Stanley McChrystal invited me to tour the battlefields at Gettysburg with students from his Yale leadership class. The group also included elite British Special Forces operators, the CEO of a large health-care system, and several former Navy SEALs. I felt way out of place among people who had made life-or-death decisions in combat zones or run big health-care systems. I had major imposter syndrome, but that discomfort was precisely why I needed to be there. That feeling of intellectual fear taught me more about my limitations than months of comfortable learning ever could. It showed me exactly what I didn't know, which is far more valuable than having your existing knowledge confirmed.

The most valuable environments make you feel slightly out of your depth. Just enough discomfort to force adaptation, not enough to drown. This feeling never goes away if you're doing it right. The topics change, but the sensation of reaching remains constant. Most people want the rewards without understanding the costs. They see the highlight reel, not the thousands of hours of invisible work. But the math of progress is simple: you get out what you put in, and the inputs are rarely glamorous.

The most powerful force in the world is compound effort over decades. One percent better today doesn't mean much. One percent better every day for a lot of years means everything.

We overestimate what we can accomplish in a day and underestimate what we can accomplish in a decade. This mismatch between our expectations and reality is why most people quit too early. Progress that matters is measured in years, not days.

Humans crave completion. We want the satisfaction of crossing finish lines. But meaningful growth doesn't work that way. The most impactful people I've met share a peculiar trait: they don't believe in "making it." They've internalized that there is no final destination, just the next challenge. Andrew Brandt joined me on a leadership retreat in Scottsdale a year ago, and said, "My life mantra is *never peak.*" Meaning, he's always striving to get a little bit better and keep climbing the mountain.

This mindset is liberating. When you stop measuring yourself against some imaginary finish line, you can appreciate the terrain you're covering. You can enjoy being perpetually unfinished. What does paying this price actually buy you? The ability to adapt when the world changes. The confidence that comes from knowing you've survived discomfort before and can do it again. Most importantly, it buys you a life that expands rather than contracts with age. Most people's worlds grow smaller as they get older. Their opinions solidify. Their willingness to try new things diminishes. The alternative is to keep paying the price of becoming. To remain perpetually under construction. To greet each day as a student rather than an expert.

The interesting thing about continuous improvement is that it follows the same mathematics as compound interest. Small, consistent inputs create disproportionate results over time.

The price of becoming is never paid in full. There's no moment when the debt is cleared, when you can stop investing and start withdrawing. The payment continues until your final day. But this ongoing cost buys something really cool: a life in continuous expansion. A mind that continues developing new rooms long after most have stopped building. The quiet confidence that comes from knowing you're still becoming, still in motion, still growing. Few are willing to pay this price consistently. But those who do purchase something beyond calculation: the privilege of never being finished, of remaining in a state of perpetual becoming. The price is high. The value is higher.

■ ■ ■

This book is an attempt to synthesize everything I've learned about walking this unpredictable path toward better leadership. After building an audience and interviewing more than seven hundred of the world's most impactful leaders, I've noticed patterns. Sometimes these patterns are hard rules, but more often they're principles that each person adapts to their own personality and circumstances.

These principles show up again and again in the lives of people who achieve lasting value, especially those who lead others.

This pattern shows up in three movements. First, you'll build your intake system. Excellent leaders don't learn accidentally. They have methods for consistently pulling in new information, perspectives, and ideas. Second, you do the work. Learning that stays theoretical is pretty much worthless. You'll sharpen how you think, how you communicate, and how you make decisions. Third, you teach what you've learned. Teaching something to someone else is how learning becomes sticky in your brain. When you teach, you discover what you actually know.

Learn. Execute. Teach. Then repeat. Here we go.

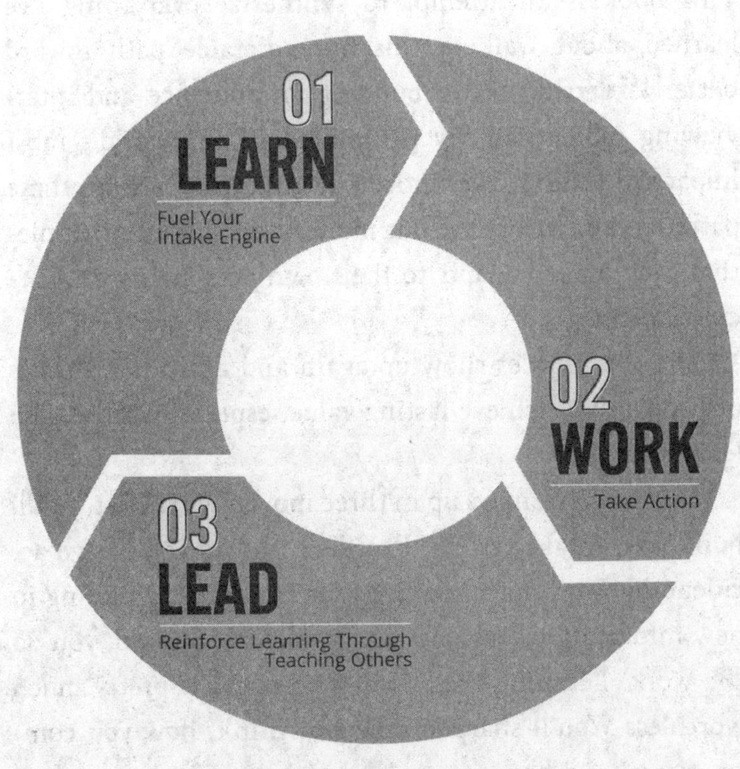
01
LEARN
Fuel Your
Intake Engine
02
WORK
Take Action
03
LEAD
Reinforce Learning Through
Teaching Others

PART I

LEARN

1

Contemplate, Copy, Create

Building Skills Through Mindful Imitation

Five young, shaggy-haired guys who shared an enthusiasm for American rock-and-roll music decided they wanted to play some songs together in hopes that others would enjoy it. On August 17, 1960, at The Indra Club in Hamburg, Germany, the band played their first gig. At the time, they were a cover band playing songs like "Long Tall Sally" by Little Richard and "Roll Over Beethoven" by Chuck Berry. For the first couple of years of the bands' existence, they would play marathon sessions sometimes lasting upwards of eight hours. These long sets forced them to expand their repertoire constantly. They'd play the same song multiple times per night, experimenting with different arrangements and developing their signature harmonies. Their lead singer later said these exhausting shows were where they really "got good."

The turning point came around 1963 into 1964. The band's producer, George Martin, encouraged them to record their own material, and songs like "I Want to Hold Your Hand" showed they were developing their own style. By 1964's "A Hard Day's Night" album, all songs were originals.

John Lennon and Paul McCartney wrote songs together as teenagers, even before Hamburg, but they initially considered these efforts amateur compared to their heroes. Yes, The Beatles (who later would slim down to four members after bassist Stuart Sutcliffe left to focus on his painting career), one of the greatest bands of all time, imitated others for years before they had the confidence and ability to find their own voice.

Not only is it common for people to imitate others while they are figuring it out, it's also useful. We don't learn how to *do the thing* by watching others. We learn by doing it. Regardless of what the thing is. It's natural and helpful to mimic others when we get started. And as we grow and evolve, we mix our unique personalities and style into it and find what makes us, us.

As a new telephonic sales rep at LexisNexis, I initially sat with others in their cubicles to listen to my teammates make calls. Eventually, when I got on the phones, I would mimic (sometimes verbatim) what I heard my colleagues saying. This happened for months before I got comfortable injecting my own personality and flair for how to speak with a prospective customer and sell them our service. As David Perell told me on *The Learning Leader Show*, "Imitate, then innovate."

FIND YOUR OWN VOICE

At some point, you move from imitating and copying others to finding your own voice. Some of the most useful insights come in moments of raw vulnerability. When I talked with Mike Maples Jr., he had lost his father just seven days earlier. The weight of that loss hung in the air as I asked him about the most valuable lessons he learned from his dad.

Mike's voice carried both the wisdom of his dad and the fresh pain of his absence as he shared: "You don't know how much time you have in this life. You gotta decide what you wanna do with the gift of your time."

These words were a son's reflection on his dad's legacy, shared during the early days of grief. The truth about honoring the gift of time hits differently when it comes from someone who's just lost their dad.

Mike continued with a quiver in his voice, "Everybody has a unique strand of DNA. No two people are exactly alike. Everyone has an opportunity to be the very best at a certain thing that's matchable to who they are. A lot of people say, 'compete by being THE best.' That's not the same thing as being your best. It's understanding what's the intersection of what you're passionate about, what you're good at, and what you can be paid for. And if you do that well, you're impossible to compete with. You won't be the best. You'll be the only."

In my years of hosting *The Learning Leader Show*, I've noticed that the guests who've made the biggest impact aren't necessarily the ones with the most impressive résumés. They're the people who've fully embraced their authentic selves and built their excellence on that foundation.

THE NO-COMFORT ZONE

Growth is uncomfortable. It has to be because real growth means leaving behind something familiar, something safe. Staying comfortable isn't neutral. It's actually a decision to stop growing.

There's a great scene from the TV show *Boy Meets World* that captures this idea perfectly. The main character, Cory Matthews, is in the garden with his wise teacher, Mr. Feeny, worried about his girlfriend, Topanga, possibly moving away. Cory doesn't like change. He wants things to stay the same. Feeny listens, then points to a flower and says: "See that flower? That flower was in a small pot in my living room, but it outgrew its surroundings, so I transplanted it here in the garden."

Cory responds, "Seems like it's doing okay."

Feeny nods. "Oh yes, it's flourishing . . . Now when I pulled the small flower out of the pot in my living room, it resisted a little, you know, tried to hang on by its roots. I had to force it out."

Cory asks, "Because you thought it would do better out here, in the world, right?"

Feeny corrects him: "No. Because I thought if I left it there, it would stop growing."

That's how it works. Staying in the pot feels good until you realize the walls are keeping you small. Cory feared that if Topanga moved, everything would fall apart. But Feeny's lesson wasn't just about a flower. It was about people, about how change, even when it feels forced on us, is often the very thing that allows us to grow.

Moving to something bigger often requires being pulled

away from what's comfortable. But eventually, you'll look back and realize the discomfort wasn't punishment; it was necessary.

GRETZKY'S OFFICE

The greatest hockey player of all time started with what many would consider a disadvantage: he was smaller than most hockey players. This is a story about adaptation. And it teaches us something useful that we often miss.

Wayne Gretzky wasn't the biggest or strongest player on the ice. In a sport dominated by physical play, this could have been a career-limiting issue. The traditional path would have been clear: bulk up, get stronger, learn to take the hits. That's what most people would have done.

But Gretzky took a different approach. From a young age, he became a student of the game. As his father Walter described, young Wayne would sit in front of the TV watching hockey games with remarkable focus. Bobby Clarke of the Philadelphia Flyers was one of the players Gretzky studied intensely. Clarke wasn't the biggest player either, but he dominated through intelligence and positioning.

Gretzky would often have a notebook out, tracking the movement of players like Clarke and the puck, and look for patterns that others missed. His father recalled how Wayne would draw diagrams of the rink, mapping out where players positioned themselves during different situations in the game.

He noticed two things that would change hockey forever:

1. Skilled players like Clarke used the corners of the rink to their advantage.
2. The space behind the net was virtually unused territory.

Instead of trying to fix his weakness (his size), Gretzky redirected it. He turned the net into a shield rather than a target. He established what became known as "Gretzky's office," the area behind the net where he could control play. He played where others didn't think to play. The results? Sixty-one NHL records, 894 goals, 1,963 assists, 2,857 points.

Gretzky didn't win by becoming someone else. He succeeded by studying the game deeply enough to find his own path through it. He didn't fight physics; he found a different way to use it. Sustainable advantages are built by finding ways to make those weaknesses irrelevant.

The next time you're faced with a limitation, remember that sometimes the best solution isn't to overcome it, but to redirect it. Gretzky's story is about the power of observation and the importance of finding your own game.

This principle extends far beyond sports. In business, you might lack the capital of established competitors, but you can create systems with fewer layers of approval that let you move faster. In careers, you might not have elite credentials, but you can build unique combinations of skills that no specialized expert possesses. In education, you might not have access to prestigious institutions, but you can develop self-directed learning habits that outpace traditional curricula. The pattern is the same: don't just play the same game better; find the part of the game others ignore. Create your own office.

THE COURAGE TO SEEK GREATNESS

Timothée Chalamet's 2025 Screen Actors Guild Best Actor acceptance speech for his portrayal of Bob Dylan in *A Complete Unknown* was all about authentic ambition. Instead of downplaying his efforts with false modesty, he acknowledged the truth: *"This was five and a half years of my life. I poured everything I had into playing this incomparable artist."*

What makes his speech so refreshing is his unapologetic declaration of purpose: *"I'm really in pursuit of greatness. I know people don't usually talk like that, but I want to be one of the greats."* By openly citing his inspirations from Daniel Day-Lewis and Viola Davis to Michael Jordan and Michael Phelps, Chalamet revealed the driving force behind his dedication.

We live in an era where performative nonchalance often masks genuine effort. This tendency to appear effortlessly successful creates a paradox: we admire achievement but scorn the visible striving required to reach it. Maybe this contradiction serves as a safety net. If we act like we didn't try that hard, rejection feels less personal.

But there's something so inspiring about those who, like Chalamet, embrace their ambitions without apology. They understand that greatness rarely happens by accident. It requires commitment, vulnerability, and the willingness to fail publicly in pursuit of something meaningful.

The brevity of his speech only amplified its impact. In recognizing his award not as validation but as *"a little more fuel . . . a little more ammo to keep going,"* he showed that true ambition is about the internal drive to continuously evolve and excel.

We should all take a page from Chalamet's playbook, acknowledging our efforts, embracing our ambitions, and understanding that while winning isn't guaranteed, the pursuit itself has intrinsic worth. The value is in who you become through the process of dedicated, intentional striving. When's the last time you admitted to someone what your real ambitions are? How often do you downplay your efforts to avoid seeming too eager, too invested? What would change if you stopped apologizing for wanting something badly? What kind of person are you becoming when you're brave enough to try, fail, and try again? What dreams are you abandoning simply because you can't guarantee the outcome?

THE PRISON, OR POTENTIAL, OF SELF-BELIEF

Few things have more influence on our outcomes than the narrow circle we draw around our potential. Most people will not venture beyond what they already think they can do. We tend to achieve almost exactly what we already decided was achievable.

This shows up everywhere. The student who "isn't good at writing" turns in mediocre essays because that's what they expected from themselves. The employee who believes they'll never make management doesn't pursue the experiences that would qualify them for a management position. Someone convinced they can't speak publicly avoids all opportunities to practice and get more comfortable. When you believe something about your abilities, you unconsciously adjust your actions to make that belief come true.

Consider the story of a sixty-one-year-old Australian potato and sheep farmer, Cliff Young, who showed up to the 1983 Sydney to Melbourne ultramarathon wearing overalls and work boots. The veteran runners laughed. Experts said completing the 543-mile race required running for eighteen hours and sleeping for six, a strategy all professional runners followed. Young, with no preconceptions about what was possible, ran at his own shuffling pace, hardly sleeping for five and a half days. He not only finished but won by a lot, breaking the previous record by nearly two days. What the professionals "knew" to be impossible blinded them to a superior approach. Young hadn't learned what couldn't be done.

The four-minute mile offers another classic example. For years, running a mile under four minutes was considered beyond human capacity. Roger Bannister finally broke it in 1954. Within weeks, others followed. Within years, hundreds had done it. The primary limitation wasn't physical. It was a collective agreement, a belief system, about where the boundary of human performance should be. Expectations can be a powerful thing. And so can confidence and belief in oneself. When Bannister stepped onto that track, he was carrying the quiet certainty that what everyone called impossible was just untested. His four-minute mile broke a false story that hundreds of other runners had been telling themselves. The funny thing about mental barriers is they're often the strongest ones we face, and the easiest ones to break once someone shows it can be done.

This works in both directions. The person who believes they'll fail takes fewer risks and creates fewer opportunities for success. The person who believes achievement is possible seeks out situations where achievement becomes probable.

REFLECTION QUESTIONS

- Who do you most admire, and what specifically about their approach could you study and practice for the next thirty days?
- What three things do you believe you "can't do" or "aren't good at" that might actually be self-imposed limitations rather than real boundaries?
- Looking at your current challenge or weakness, how could you redirect it rather than trying to overcome it directly? What would your "office behind the net" look like?
- What's the intersection of what energizes you, what you're naturally good at, and what people would pay you for? Be specific.
- What ambitious goal are you embarrassed to say out loud, and why does admitting your pursuit of greatness feel uncomfortable?

Take Action

- **Find someone worth copying, then copy them relentlessly.** The fastest way to get good at anything is to study someone who's already figured it out. Pick one person whose work you respect. For the next thirty days, imitate their methods exactly. Don't try to be original. Originality comes later, after you understand the basics.

- **Carry a notebook everywhere (or write notes on your phone).** Most people go through life half-asleep. They miss the small moments that contain big insights. Start writing down things you notice each day that other people ignore. The person who pays attention to details that others miss will have an advantage.

- **Answer three questions honestly.** What makes you lose track of time? What do people consistently ask for your help with? What would you do for free because you enjoy it that much? The intersection of these three answers is where you'll find work that feels like play.

- **Start using your weaknesses.** Everyone has limitations. Most people waste energy trying to fix them. Smart people figure out how to make their weaknesses irrelevant. For example, if you're not a natural public speaker, become the go-to person for one-to-one client relationships or written communication. Or if you're introverted in a sales environment, don't worry about schmoozing at happy hours, and become the person who solves complex technical problems for clients.

- **Study fields that have nothing to do with yours.** The best ideas come from combining insights from different areas. Spend time learning about something completely unrelated to your work. A biologist studying economics might discover something neither pure biologist nor pure economist would see.

- **Question what you think you can't do.** Most of your limitations exist only in your head. Write down three things you've always believed you're bad at. Then do one small thing this week to test whether that's actually true. You might surprise yourself.

- **Own your ambitions.** Pretending you don't care about success won't protect you from failure, but it will guarantee mediocrity. Tell someone what you're actually trying to accomplish. Say it out loud. The people who achieve big things aren't embarrassed about wanting them.

2

Curiosity Compounds

Conversation and Exploration

I was lost. It was a cool morning in March 2019. I had been to New York City a few times over the years, but this visit was different. I was there to meet with one of my creative heroes, Brian Koppelman, creator of the TV show *Billions* and the movie *Rounders*. I texted with him to get the updated address (where we were going to record) and eventually got to his office after a few wrong turns. During the interview he said something to me which has stuck years later: *"Keep following your curiosity and obsessions with great rigor."*

This resonated deeply because Koppelman was recognizing the very quality that led me to start *The Learning Leader Show* in the first place, a deep curiosity about impactful leaders and how they sustain excellence; it also seemed to be indicating that curiosity was the secret ingredient for his own career success as well.

Over the past decade, I've learned that curiosity is a useful way to show love and respect. When you genuinely care about someone's story, ask thoughtful questions, listen carefully to their answers, and then ask even better follow-ups, you build deeper, more meaningful connections. You also learn more than you do if you're talking the whole time. This mindset has helped me forge life-changing relationships and elevate my career higher than I thought possible. And it's one that anyone can develop.

INQUISITIVE

Curiosity is a valuable skill disguised as a personality trait. It might be the most underrated asset in your life. Being genuinely interested in a lot of topics can help you develop a mental tool kit that lets you see connections that others miss, which is a competitive advantage.

If you think about it, most innovation comes from connecting existing ideas in ways nobody thought possible before. When you're curious about everything from quantum physics to Renaissance art, your brain creates a database of patterns that start talking to each other in surprising ways.

This happens slowly, then all at once, like compound interest but for your brain.

I've noticed something fascinating about adaptability too. People who regularly explore unfamiliar territory develop comfort with discomfort. They've trained their minds to say, "I don't know yet" instead of "I can't figure this out." This subtle difference changes your approach to new challenges. I saw this recently when my daughters and I did an escape room. What struck me was their complete inability to recognize when they should give up. They approached each dead end like it was just another data point, not a reason to quit. And then did that all the way until we made it out. It was cool to witness.

Empathy works the same way. Reading widely about different cultures and perspectives diversifies your emotional portfolio. You start recognizing that people's behaviors make sense given their unique histories, even when those behaviors seem crazy to you at first.

Hedy Lamarr was a movie star from Hollywood's golden era, but her curiosity created something much more lasting. During World War II, she developed a frequency-hopping signal that enemy forces couldn't jam. Her Hollywood friends probably thought this hobby was weird. Why was a beautiful actress obsessed with radio frequencies? But that odd combination of interests led to technology that later became fundamental to Bluetooth, GPS, and Wi-Fi. Being interested in seemingly unrelated fields, entertainment and military communication, created something neither field would have developed alone.

I've found this in my own life, too. The most valuable skill isn't expertise in any one thing. It's the ability to learn new things. And learning becomes easier when you're genuinely interested in everything around you. An inquisitive life isn't just more useful. It's more fun. The world becomes an endless source of wonder. Each day offers new discoveries that compound over time into a richer existence, which is what we're all really after.

■ ■ ■

Connecting ideas creates value. Together, the cell phone, the iPod, and the PalmPilot became the iPhone. In the same way, connecting diverse minds can be just as powerful. Over a decade of hosting *The Learning Leader Show* podcast, I've discovered that curious people from diverse backgrounds can combine in powerful and unpredictable ways. Looking back, I can trace most of my adult learning and growth to deliberately creating collisions of curious people.

I run Learning Leader Circles every year. When assembling these mastermind groups, I purposely mix industries, job titles, geography, and so on. A fifty-two-year-old tech CEO from India, a forty-year-old lawyer from New Jersey, and a high school football coach from Virginia create interesting conversations. The more disparate the life experiences and worldviews, the more rapid and pronounced the benefits of connection.

Surprisingly, conversing with top performers isn't the hard part of leveraging this tool. CEOs, athletes, and artists are usually easier to talk to than that distant cousin at Thanksgiving. It's their primary job to connect, so they're good at it. The challenge for ambitious learning leaders involves finding the right people to meet, asking for their time, and overcoming the irrational fear of rejection or looking foolish. We know how valuable these connections can be, yet we still hesitate to reach out.

The brute force approach can work. For the first few years of my professional career, I made sixty cold calls a day as a sales rep. But there are better ways to master the art of connection and conversation. Curiosity, being genuinely fascinated by people and their stories, provides a foundation for a more interesting future.

■ ■ ■

Look at the California Redwoods. They can grow to be more than three hundred feet tall. You would assume these majestic giants would have deep roots to support their height. However, instead of growing down, their roots grow out, enmeshing themselves with one another. Interconnectedness allows each tree to reach staggering heights. This is why we never see a lone redwood. They thrive in a grove, bound together. (I learned this from a conversation with bestselling author Brad Stulberg.)

This principle is also demonstrated in The Harvard Study of Adult Development, one of the longest-running studies of adult life ever conducted, following participants for over eighty years. Its primary purpose is to answer the question, "What leads to a happy life?" The main finding has been surprisingly straightforward: good relationships keep us happier and healthier. The study's associate director, Marc Schulz, summarized it well on *The Learning Leader Show*: *"Relationships are at the core of human flourishing. The clearest message that we get from this 80-year study is this: Great relationships keep us happier and healthier. Period."*

WORD OF THE YEAR: *CONNECTION*

In late 2024, I decided to focus on one word for 2025. Not that other things weren't important, but I wanted to go hard in 2025 in one specific area. The word I chose was *connection*. The best moments in life happen when I'm building and deepening relationships with high-character, highly accomplished people. So, I booked an Airbnb, flights, lift tickets, rentals, and decided that January 1, 2025, we would be on a mountain in Utah skiing as a family. That's how we spent the first seven days of the new year. I'd never done that before. It ended up being my favorite family vacation we've ever had. Three of our teenagers learned to ski, and our youngest got to show her stuff to her older sisters after learning the year prior. We laughed a lot, cried a little, shared many meals, lived in a small house for the week, went up ski lifts, had deep conversations, learned more about the lingo of high schoolers, got made fun of, had two flight cancellations, spent five hours in a Delta club, and at the end of it, all of them said, "Can we please do this again soon?" Does it get any better than that? I'm not sure if it does.

I also rented a house in Scottsdale, Arizona, for three days at the end of January. My intention was to ask twelve high-character, growth-focused, family men to be together. Share great meals, do challenging hikes, and focus on having deep, single-threaded conversations. We did all of those things. Some of the guys already knew each other, but most had never met. Several factors helped create *connection* during our men's leadership retreat:

- We all stayed in the same house. Get a house with enough beds for everyone.
- We ate all of our meals at the house. I hired a chef to ensure the food was great. By the second meal, we were

sharing Dad jokes along with deeply personal (and often painful) stories about loved ones dying . . . and everything in between.

- As the organizer, I was very intentional about the guest list. A few mandatory qualities for me in my selection of people:
  - » High-character dudes who others would enjoy being around. There were no seating charts. I wanted it not to matter who you sat next to at dinner. Regardless, it was going to be an interesting, curious, thoughtful person.
  - » Highly accomplished. A few guys had built billion-dollar businesses and flew there on their private planes. A couple of young military guys had been all over the world (including one who had been on every continent by the time he was twenty-three). The best way to get others to invite you to an event is to live an interesting life and do something meaningful that positively impacts the world (defend our country, start a business that creates lots of jobs, publish helpful books, etc.).
  - » A good hang. If you need to make sure that others *know* you're the smartest person in the room, then we don't want you in the room. Nobody likes that guy. It all stems from insecurity, and it's unattractive. Don't do that. Figure out where that insecurity comes from and then stop bragging about how awesome you are.
- Single-threaded conversations. Design moments for relaxed, casual conversation in small groups as well as formal sessions with all twelve participants focusing on one specific topic (chosen by the group). Only one per-

son talks and the rest listen; then another person follows up on the previous point. And so on.

- Do something hard together. I hired a local hiking guide to take us on two big hikes, one at sunset and one at sunrise. During the hike, most guys paired off in twos and had great one-on-one conversations. Then we got to the top and had just done the hard thing together. How to get close to another person? Laugh together, cry together, and do something hard together. Check. Check. Check.

YOUR MOVE

Now, it's your turn. Pick one word for the year that will boost your curiosity, lead you into new domains, and create new connections.

When you try to focus on everything, you focus on nothing. One word can change this. It becomes your filter for decisions, your magnet for opportunities. Your word is probably already there. Maybe it's adventure, create, learn, serve, health, or presence. The right word often feels exciting and slightly scary. It makes you think: "If I really lived this out, everything would improve."

Action: Choose your word this week. Ask, "What do I most want to cultivate?" Circle the word that makes your heart beat faster. Get specific. If it's *adventure*, what adventures? If it's *create*, what will you create? Write down three things you'll actually do. Then . . . book the trip, sign up for the class, send the email. My ski trip started by booking the Airbnb and buying lift tickets.

Here's what tends to happen: when you follow genuine

curiosity into new domains, you often become more interesting. Interesting people attract other interesting people. Soon, you're having conversations you never would have had with people you never would have met. That Arizona retreat? Twelve people who didn't know each other built the foundation for lifelong friendships because we all showed up curious.

At the end of the year, you'll be somewhere. You might as well choose where. So, what's your word? Write it down. Then make the first move to make it real.

WHO YOU LISTEN TO SHAPES WHAT YOU DO

Connection is important for its own sake, but it also has a big effect on the outcomes in our individual lives.

In 1976, a young engineer named Steve Wozniak designed the first personal computer in his free time. It was just a hobby, something he worked on for fun. At the time, computers were massive machines owned by governments and corporations. The idea that an individual would want one seemed absurd. Wozniak showed his design to his boss at Hewlett-Packard, expecting some encouragement. Instead, HP told him it was a waste of time. They didn't see the potential, and they certainly didn't think anyone would buy it. He offered them the rights to his design five different times. They rejected it every time.

Most people in his position would have stopped there. When enough smart people tell you something won't work, it's easy to believe them. But Wozniak had a friend who saw things differently. Steve Jobs wasn't an engineer, but he understood something Wozniak's bosses didn't:

just because an idea sounds crazy today doesn't mean it won't be obvious tomorrow. Jobs convinced Wozniak to ignore HP's rejection and build the computer himself. They started Apple in a garage with no outside support. The same product that HP had dismissed became the foundation of a company that would change the world.

Sam Altman (CEO of OpenAI) once said, "Surround yourself with people who will make you more ambitious, more inquisitive, shift your perspective more. 98% of people will try to pull you back and say that's a little bit too crazy, a little bit too out there, too ambitious."

Wozniak could have listened to the people who told him personal computers were a dead end. Instead, he listened to Jobs, who pushed him to think bigger. The difference between Apple being an idea and Apple becoming a trillion-dollar company came down to whom Wozniak chose to listen to. Most people are cautious by nature. They want to avoid failure, so they encourage you to play it safe. They don't want to see you take risks they wouldn't take themselves. But history shows that what seems too ambitious today often becomes obvious in hindsight.

Who you surround yourself with shapes how you see the world. If you spend time with people who dismiss big ideas, you will start to lower your own expectations. If you surround yourself with people who push boundaries, you will start to believe that pushing boundaries is normal. The best ideas often look crazy at first. The key is making sure you're around people who see potential instead of limits.

Here's what happened when researchers decided to look at something nobody had looked at before. The Framingham Heart Study had been tracking thousands of people since 1948, collecting mountains of health data. But buried in their filing cabinets were handwritten administrative sheets that tracked something else: who was friends with whom. When researchers finally examined this social network data spanning thirty-two years and 12,067 people, they discovered that clusters of happy and unhappy people were visible throughout the network, with relationships extending up to three degrees of separation. Your friend's friend's friend could predict your well-being better than many factors we typically obsess over.

The numbers tell a story that defies common sense. If your friend became obese, your chances of becoming obese increased by 57 percent. But here's where it gets weird: you were 20 percent more likely to become obese if a friend of a friend became obese, even if the connecting friend stayed exactly the same weight. Somehow, behaviors were jumping across people like an invisible contagion. Think about what this means. We spend enormous energy optimizing our diets, our exercise routines, our supplements. But the Framingham data suggests that simply having a happy friend who lives within a mile increases your probability of being happy by 25 percent. The most powerful health intervention might be simply choosing the right people to surround ourselves with. Those around you aren't just witnesses to your life choices. They're co-authors of them, whether you realize it or not.

SURROUND YOURSELF WITH "WHY NOT?"

The greatest lessons come from moments when life strips away all pretense and forces you to confront reality in its rawest form. This is what happened to filmmaker Kevin Smith. He's the creator of cult classics like *Clerks*, *Mallrats*, and *Chasing Amy*.

During a Q&A session for his program *Burn in Hell*, Smith shared a story about his dad. "I got a phone call at like five-thirty in the morning. It was my brother. He's like, 'You gotta get down to the hospital on Walnut right now. Dad's in the hospital.'"

When he got to the emergency room, Smith witnessed something that would haunt him: *"I saw something so horrifying. Something I had never seen before. It was my mother crying, but not like crying. I've seen her cry. This was different. This is the crying one does when someone's fucking scared big time. When a life is hanging in the balance. She couldn't put words together."*

"I go into the emergency room and they said, 'Donald Smith. I'm sorry he passed.' They took me into the room, there's my father laying on a gurney, just dead."

Kevin spent a few minutes in the room and then went outside to have a cigarette and collect himself. His brother shared details that would forever alter Smith's perspective.

"My brother comes out and he said, 'Dad died screaming.' I was like, What? What do you mean? 'He woke up, and he was kicking the sheets off him and screaming about being on fire. He was so hot, he wanted water. The screaming got louder and louder. It reached a fever pitch, and then he died.'"

This hit Smith "like a Mack truck." Not just that his father had died, but that he had died in distress. In pain. Without dignity or peace.

The cruel irony wasn't lost on Smith. His father had

lived modestly, prioritizing others above himself. "I remember asking him once, 'Dad, what were your dreams?' And he was just like, 'Well, I wanted to get married and have kids.'

"He was a good dude," Smith continued. "He worked at the post office his whole life just to pay for the family. He didn't necessarily like working for the post office or believe in the mail, but it was what he needed to do to pay for his wife and his kids."

In that moment, Smith confronted an uncomfortable truth: his dad had postponed his own dreams and desires to provide stability for his family. He had played by the rules. He had done everything "right." And his reward? A painful death that offered no acknowledgment of his sacrifice.

This realization crystallized a philosophy that would guide the rest of his life: "And I remember thinking, in this world, where even a good man is going to die screaming, *there's no point in not trying to achieve every dream that I have.* This is my eventual end. One day, that's it. The best thing to do is to try to pack that life with as much wonderfulness, fun, and productivity." If playing it safe offers no protection from suffering, why not pursue what brings you joy and fulfillment? If the end result is the same regardless, the journey becomes everything.

Through his death, Donald Smith gave his son the clarity to see life for what it truly is: brief, unpredictable, and too precious to waste on unfulfilling obligations or unexplored passions.

This is a wake-up call for anyone postponing their dreams for some hypothetical future that may never arrive. It's a reminder that safety is largely an illusion, and that the only true security comes from having lived according to your deepest values. As Kevin Smith discovered through tragedy, there truly is "no point in not trying to achieve every dream that I have." The only logical response to our mortality is to maximize every moment we're given.

THE BADDEST THING I'D EVER SEEN

The hidden power of excellence is that it's contagious. Dave Matthews has often reflected that Carter Beauford's brilliance on the drums makes him a better musician, songwriter, and performer. Excellence transforms a team, creating an environment where mediocrity can't survive.

> The reason I went to Carter (Beauford) was not because I needed a drummer, but because I thought he was the baddest thing I'd ever seen, and LeRoi (Moore), it wasn't because I desperately wanted a saxophone, it was because this guy just blew my mind. At this jazz place I used to bartend at, Miller's, I would just sit back and watch him. I would be serving the musicians fat whiskeys, and they'd be getting more and more hosed, but no matter how much, he used to still blow my mind. And it was the sense that everyone played from their heart. And when we got together and they asked, "What do you want the music to sound like?" I said, "I know this is a song I wrote, and I like what you guys play, so I want you to play the way you react to my song." There was a lot of breaking our inhibitions.

This reflects a truth that applies well beyond music: excellence attracts excellence, and when given room to operate, it compounds.

Most people get this backward. They hire for specific skills to fill specific roles, then micromanage the process. But extraordinary outcomes rarely come from ordinary approaches. What's equally important to the Dave Matthews Band's success is that Carter Beauford and LeRoi Moore weren't just virtuosos; they were also great teammates and collaborators. The band's chemistry comes from this rare combination of exceptional skill and high character. In addition to being wowed by their skill, Dave had spent time with them at Miller's, getting to know them as people.

When you bring in teammates who are genuinely exceptional both in their abilities and in how they work with others, a few important things happen: first, you benefit from skills and perspectives you didn't even know you needed. Carter Beauford brought drumming techniques that Dave couldn't have specifically requested because he wouldn't have known how to ask for them. Second, people perform at their highest level when they feel ownership. Dave didn't tell his bandmates how to play; he invited them to react to his songs in their own way. This created space for genuine creativity. Third, excellence is contagious. When people work alongside others who are truly exceptional, they naturally elevate their own performance. Standards rise without anyone needing to enforce them. Fourth, character qualities like humility, generosity, and teamwork allow that individual brilliance to become something greater than the sum of its parts.

Without these qualities, even virtuosos can't create something that lasts.

The greatest teams in any field combine world-class talent with the right personal qualities:

- Listening and responding to others rather than just waiting for their turn
- Supporting teammates' growth and success
- Maintaining humility despite exceptional abilities
- Bringing positive energy that elevates everyone around them
- Putting collective success above personal recognition

Few things are more powerful than a collection of talented, collaborative people who feel the freedom to do their best work. This is about understanding that character is what turns individual brilliance into collective greatness. So, the question isn't just "Who are the most talented people I can find?" but also "Who has the character to make others better?" and "Am I creating an environment where that combination can fully express itself?"

What's made the Dave Matthews Band special is the magic that happens when those exceptional talents, who also happen to be great humans, are allowed to interact freely, creating something none of them could have done alone. And from that early decision Dave made in 1991, the band has since grossed over $1 billion in ticket sales at concerts, delighting fans for decades with their unique sound and obvious love for performing together, as evidenced by the giant smiles on their faces while onstage.

REFLECTION QUESTIONS

- What topic, completely unrelated to your work, has been catching your attention lately, and what would happen if you followed that curiosity obsessively for a month?
- Who are the five people you spend the most time with, and do they encourage your biggest ideas or unconsciously talk you out of them?
- When you have an exciting new idea, who do you tell first? Do they respond with "Why not?" or immediately list reasons it won't work?
- What's one meaningful gathering you could organize this year that would bring together interesting people from different backgrounds and industries?
- If you're honest with yourself, what aspects of your own happiness and emotional health have you been expecting others to manage for you?

Take Action

- **Follow one curiosity obsessively for thirty days.** Pick something that genuinely fascinates you but feels unrelated to your work. Read about it, watch videos, talk to experts. Your brain will start connecting this new knowledge to everything else you know in ways you can't predict. And then share what you've learned with someone else.

- **Ask better questions in every conversation.** Most people wait for their turn to talk. Instead, listen for what someone really cares about, then ask why it matters to them. Follow up with "What surprised you about that?" The person who asks the best questions learns the most.

- **Every week, reach out to one person you admire.** Share what you learned from their work. High-performing people are easier to reach than you think, and genuine appreciation opens more doors than clever pitches.

- **Create space for unexpected connections.** Join a group, attend an event, or start a conversation where you're the least experienced person in the room. Discomfort means you're in the right place. The most valuable insights come from perspectives you wouldn't encounter otherwise.

- **Document what you notice.** Carry a notebook or use your phone to capture interesting observations, overheard conversations, or random thoughts. Your curiosity gets stronger when you pay attention to what catches your attention.
- **Audit your inner circle ruthlessly.** Write down a list of the people you spend the most time with. Do they encourage your biggest ideas or talk you out of them? Ambitious people need to be around other ambitious people.
- **Plan one meaningful gathering this year.** Bring together six to twelve interesting people for a dinner, weekend trip, or shared experience. Mix industries and backgrounds on purpose. The conversations that happen when curious people collide often change everyone involved.
- **Invest in your own emotional health.** Happy people build better relationships and attract better opportunities. Whether that's therapy, exercise, meditation, or just saying no to things that drain you, your external success depends on your internal state.
- **Start something that forces you to meet new people.** Launch a podcast, organize a book club, volunteer for a cause you care about. When you create value for others, you naturally attract interesting people who want to help you succeed.

3

Question Everything

Challenging Assumptions for Growth

In 1985, an Apple middle manager named Donna Dubinsky faced a decision that would define her career: challenge Steve Jobs or stay quiet. Jobs, then chairman of the board, had proposed eliminating Apple's six U.S. warehouses and shifting to a just-in-time production system. Computers would be assembled on demand and shipped overnight via FedEx.

On paper, the idea seemed innovative. Reduce inventory costs. Streamline operations. Cut expenses. The kind of efficiency Silicon Valley celebrates. But Dubinsky, who managed Apple's distribution, saw a fatal flaw. She understood something Jobs missed: the actual day-to-day reality of how Apple's business worked.

"In my mind, Apple being successful depended on distribution being successful," she said.

The company wasn't shipping integrated products. The Apple II, which generated the most revenue, required components from multiple sources. Computers arrived from one facility, monitors from another, disk drives from somewhere else. These parts came together at distribution centers before reaching small, undercapitalized retailers who couldn't afford to maintain inventory themselves. Jobs's plan ignored this reality. It wasn't just a minor oversight. It threatened the entire business.

What Dubinsky did next deserves our attention. Rather than comply with the powerful founder, she delivered an ultimatum: give her thirty days to develop a counterproposal, or she would resign. Dubinsky had done her homework. She had savings to fall back on. She knew the business deeply. And most importantly, she cared more about doing what was right for Apple than protecting her position. The result? Her proposal prevailed. Rather than getting fired, she earned a promotion to run an Apple software subsidiary. Later, she would go on to become CEO of Palm Computing and co-found Handspring, creating some of the first smartphones.

Having the conviction to stand behind your expertise when it matters most is a superpower.

Organizations fail because smart people stay silent. What made Donna Dubinsky exceptional was her willingness to risk her position to protect the company she served. She understood that true loyalty sometimes means challenging leadership, not blindly following it. My friend Brook Cupps has a core value on his basketball team of being *unified*. He defines that as *speaking and acting with urgency*. When I asked him what *unified* actually looks like in practice, he gave a great example: "Seeing a teammate not touch a line during wind sprints and not speaking up is a selfish act. If a teammate is not upholding the standard, and you don't say something, you are being selfish. *You are choosing your comfort over the standards of the team.* Don't be selfish."

In our careers, we'll all face moments when we must choose between comfortable silence and uncomfortable truth. Most choose silence. The path to exceptional outcomes often requires the latter. The next time you see something wrong in your organization, think of Donna Dubinsky. Consider that your decision to speak up might not end your career but elevate it. This is growth in its most practical form. Every time you choose difficult honesty over easy silence, you build the muscle that separates good careers from great ones. You're proving to yourself and others that you can handle the bigger problems that come with bigger opportunities. The conviction to stand behind your expertise when it matters most is surprisingly rare. We want to work with someone who will tell them when they're about to make a serious mistake. Be that person.

SPACE RACE

The greatest challengers do years of homework.

The seeds of NASA's success in the Space Race were planted decades before takeoff, in the habits of a young girl in White Sulphur Springs, West Virginia. Katherine Johnson counted everything. Length of the road. Steps to church. Dishes in the sink. Each tally was a deposit in what would become the most valuable account in America's space program: deep mathematical understanding.

Small habits multiply over time in ways that are hard

to see in the moment but become obvious in retrospect. By the time she was thirteen, Katherine had already established her daily deposit schedule by taking advanced math classes three years ahead of her peers. By fifteen, she was in college. By eighteen, she had graduated summa cum laude with majors in mathematics and French.

But the real power of her approach was in the consistency of her learning system. When others rushed to finish calculations, Katherine built checklists. When others accepted given formulas, she derived them from first principles. When others stayed quiet, she asked questions: "Is there a law against it?"

By 1962, Katherine had developed such a reputation for accuracy that John Glenn refused to fly his historic orbital mission until she had personally verified the calculations. In an era when electronic computers were new and uncertain, Glenn trusted the human computer who had spent decades depositing knowledge into her mathematical account. The greatest returns in Johnson's career came from what seemed like an unnecessary habit: *questioning everything*. At NASA, when presented with calculations, she would ask, "Why? Where did that number come from?" Other computers simply ran the numbers. Katherine built understanding.

Katherine Johnson's success derived from building systems that made excellence inevitable. Count everything. Question everything. And then understand it. These weren't just habits; they were a comprehensive *system* for compound learning.

By the time American astronauts were reaching for the moon, Katherine Johnson had accumulated decades of mathematical excellence through thousands of small, daily acts of curiosity and rigor. The space program reaped the rewards of her lifelong dedication to learning.

TO THE SKIES

Many people have heard of the Wright brothers; very few have heard of Otto Lilienthal. There's a reason for that.

Otto Lilienthal was a German aviation pioneer known as the Glider King. He was the first person to make repeated, successful glider flights (over 2,000 of them). His key contribution was proving that curved wing surfaces generated more lift than flat ones. He published detailed data tables about air pressure on curved surfaces in his 1889 book *Birdflight as the Basis of Aviation*. Lilienthal's systematic approach to flight testing and his published photographs of successful glides inspired many early aviation pioneers, including the Wright brothers. Wilbur Wright noted: "Of all the men who attacked the flying problem in the 19th century, Otto Lilienthal was easily the most important."

Orville and Wilbur Wright developed a curious, questioning mindset while growing up in Dayton, Ohio. Their dad, Milton Wright, understood the power of curiosity and helped grow this skill within his boys by maintaining a large library at home, and he encouraged lots of reading. When his sons showed interest in a topic, he'd help them find relevant books. As a bishop who traveled frequently, he'd bring back mechanical toys and intellectual puzzles for his children. A toy helicopter he brought back in 1878 fascinated young Wilbur and Orville. Most importantly, he encouraged questioning and independent thinking. He taught them to form their own conclusions rather than accepting conventional wisdom. His motto was "If I were you, I would examine it for myself."

One of the most telling examples of the Wright brothers' questioning mindset was their investigation of Otto Lilienthal's data. Lilienthal had published widely accepted tables about air pressure on curved surfaces. In 1901, when the Wrights' glider wasn't performing as Lilienthal's calculations predicted, they questioned his data. They built a wind tunnel to test wing designs and discovered Lilienthal's measurements were incorrect. Their questioning revealed that the accepted lift equation of the time was wrong by over 50 percent. This discovery was crucial to developing their successful wing design.

Wilbur Wright later wrote: "Having set out with absolute faith in the existing scientific data, we were driven to doubt one thing after another, until finally, after two years of experiment, we cast it all aside and decided to rely entirely upon our own investigations." This questioning of established "facts" directly led to the first successful powered flight.

The Wright brothers' deep curiosity and questioning mindset was critical to their triumphs. And the research suggests that this approach to life has compounding effects.

THE SCIENTIFIC BENEFITS OF CURIOSITY

Curiosity and intellectual rigor are not only for history makers and CEOs. They are tools for everyday people who want to increase the quality of their lives. Science has a lot to say about the subject.

The Seattle Longitudinal Study is one of our best long-term studies on cognitive development. Started in 1956 by K. Warner Schaie and now continuing under Sherry L. Willis, it has followed participants for over sixty years. Key findings specifically about curiosity and cognitive engagement show:

1. Participants who stayed intellectually curious and engaged showed less cognitive decline compared to those who didn't.
2. Even more fascinating, they found evidence that active curiosity could help reverse some cognitive decline. When participants increased their intellectual engagement through learning new skills or pursuing new interests, their scores improved.

The Max Planck Institute research, led by Martin Lövdén, revealed something notable about the brain: learning completely new skills in older age (sixty plus) led to increased gray matter volume in memory-related brain regions. This wasn't just about maintaining existing knowledge; it was the result of novel learning and exploration. A compelling example from their work involved teaching older adults to juggle. Those who approached the task with curiosity and persistence not only learned faster, but also showed measurable changes in brain structure. This demonstrates that the brain maintains significant plasticity when engaged through curiosity.

Todd Kashdan's research at George Mason University has shown that curiosity serves as a significant predictor of:

- Greater life satisfaction
- Better relationship quality
- Higher achievement in both work and personal goals

Curiosity and questioning everything are the choices we make every day. When we choose to stay curious, to ask one more question, to dig a little deeper, we're investing in our future selves. The dividends come in the form of unexpected opportunities and moments of insight that could change everything. I've watched and participated in big deals that have emerged from simple follow-up questions. I've seen lifelong friendships form because someone cared enough to ask "Why?" I've witnessed careers transformed because of a willingness to explore the unknown. The beauty of curiosity is that it's always available to us.

Questions compound indefinitely. Ask why a store puts candy at the checkout counter, and you learn about impulse buying. Ask why impulse buying works, and you learn about willpower. Ask why willpower fails, and you learn about human psychology. Each answer creates new questions, and each new question has the potential to change how you see everything else.

THE POWER OF GOOD QUESTIONS

Some of the most surprising scientific insights come from asking simple questions about everyday things. When Richard Feynman wondered why rubber bands become warm when stretched, his investigation revealed how the invisible world of molecules creates the forces we feel in everyday objects. The question seemed trivial at first, the kind a child might ask. But that was its power. Edwin Land's three-year-old daughter asked him, "Why do we have to wait for the picture?" while using a camera. Instead of dismissing that question as a child's impatience, he toyed with it. It led to the invention of instant photography and Polaroid.

In each case, the initial question wasn't necessarily sophisticated. But it was specific enough to guide investigation while being open-ended enough to allow for unexpected discoveries.

The physicist Isidor Rabi once explained why he became a scientist. While other mothers would ask their children, "Did you learn anything today?" his mother would ask, "Did you ask any good questions today?" The difference is subtle but important. One treats knowledge as something to be passively received. The other treats it as something to be actively pursued.

Pulitzer Prize–winning historian David Hackett Fischer observed that questions *"are the engines of intellect, cerebral machines that convert curiosity into controlled inquiry."* Great questions arise out of genuine curiosity. And to get to the truth, they need to be asked without bias Where people get this wrong is when they approach a person or a topic with a preexisting belief and have no desire to disprove that belief. In fact, it should be the opposite. The leaders I've met who ask the best questions share a few qualities:

- **Genuine intellectual curiosity:** a deep, sincere desire to understand rather than just confirm what they already believe. This means approaching topics with wonder and openness rather than trying to prove themselves right.
- **Comfort with uncertainty and not knowing:** good questions often come from embracing what they don't understand rather than hiding it. Being willing to say, "I

don't know, but I'd like to understand" opens up deeper inquiry.

- **Patience:** quality questions rarely emerge instantly. They require a person to sit with a topic, turning it over in their mind and letting understanding evolve. Initial questions are often superficial; deeper questions emerge as a person engages more fully with a subject.
- **Intellectual humility:** Shane Snow (author of *Dream Teams*) told me that this is the most important skill in a leader who sustains excellence over time: the ability to sit between gullibility and stubbornness. Leaders who do this recognize that their current understanding may be incomplete or incorrect. This allows them to question their own assumptions and biases rather than just accepting them.
- **Attentiveness:** paying close attention to details, inconsistencies, and patterns. Many good questions arise from noticing what doesn't quite fit or make sense within a person's current understanding.

These leaders have a mindset that values questions *in and of themselves*, not just for the answers they might produce. They understand that the quality of their questions often matters more than quick answers, as better questions lead to deeper insights and understanding.

NARROWING YOUR FOCUS

A lesson in simplification came to me from coaching an all-girls flag football team competing in an all-boys league. One of my players, Sammi, was among the fastest girls on the team. Sammi, however, was so scared of carrying the ball that she was the only player on the team who begged not to do it. But here's the cool thing about fear: it can turn our greatest strengths into unused assets.

As a former quarterback, I understood something crucial about performance under pressure: complexity is the enemy of execution. So, I gave Sammi the simplest possible instruction: "Get the ball, run as fast as you can to the endzone. I don't care if they pull your flag in the backfield, a few yards downfield, or anywhere. You get the ball and go. As fast as you can." We stripped away every complex element of football and reduced it to a single focus point that leveraged her core strength. Nothing about reading defenders, following blockers, or protecting the ball. Just run.

The result? Sammi blasted past the first defender, then the second, and sprinted forty yards for a touchdown. Her teammates went nuts. It was awesome. They knew what she had overcome and were pumped up for her!

I learned this principle during my own playing days as a quarterback. The position involves managing ten teammates, getting the signal for the play from the coach on the sidelines, calling the play, reading eleven defenders, making pre-snap adjustments, then executing the play at a high level. It's a mental load that can overwhelm anyone. My solution? A simple three-word mantra: "Execute my job." This narrowing made the complex feel manageable. This goes way beyond sports. When I'm facing any daunting challenge now, whether it's giving a big keynote speech or leading an initiative that could impact a lot of people, I return to that same mantra: "Execute my job. Execute my job. Execute my job." There's something about the word *execute* that helps me get it done.

When complexity rises, the answer is to subtract until you're left with only what's essential, until the challenge becomes simple enough to act on. This approach gives you permission to ignore everything else. And in a world of endless complexity, the ability to ignore well is a useful skill.

How can you apply this? Start by identifying a current challenge: maybe it's launching a new product, managing a difficult project, or making a career transition. Then ask yourself: What's your equivalent of "just run as fast as you can"? What's the one thing you do well that, if focused on exclusively, could make a difference? Maybe you're an excellent writer drowning in the complexities of building a business: make writing good copy your singular focus and ignore everything else for now. Maybe you're a talented programmer overwhelmed by startup logistics: focus solely on building your product and defer the rest. Write your simplified focus on a sticky note, just as I use "Execute my job," and let it be your North Star when complexity threatens to overwhelm you. Remember, you don't need to solve every problem today. There will always be more work to do. Identify a strength area, focus, solve it, and then, move on to the next problem to solve.

PERPETUAL DISSATISFACTION

The funny thing about winning is how quickly it becomes normal. One day you're celebrating a milestone, and by the next morning, it feels like the baseline. This psychological quirk is a useful feature in high performers. The most remarkable leaders have a relationship with success that looks dysfunctional from the outside but proves invaluable in practice: they win, they acknowledge it a little bit, then they immediately start working on what's next. They have allergic reactions to complacency.

Gokul Rajaram, who's had front-row seats watching several founders build big companies, noticed this pattern:

> I've now closely worked with/for several founders of $25B+ companies, and one characteristic I've observed in all of them: PERPETUAL DISSATISFACTION WITH THE STATE OF THE COMPANY. They are not satisfied, even as the company hits its goals, scales and grows, and even as most employees/investors feel happy with where the company is at . . . they ALWAYS have a list of 5–6 things that team or person could be doing better.

In the military defense industry, where the stakes involve human lives rather than just quarterly earnings, Marillyn Hewson applied this same principle at Lockheed Martin. After delivering F-35 fighter jets ahead of schedule and under budget, something practically unheard of in defense contracting, Hewson didn't throw a party. She launched a comprehensive review of the entire production process. "You can never rest on your laurels in this business," she told *The Washington Post.* While everyone was patting Lockheed on the back, Hewson was obsessing over driving costs down further, improving maintenance, and enhancing training systems. Under her watch, the cost per F-35 dropped by more than 60 percent from early models. As she once said, "The solutions to yesterday's problems aren't going to be the solutions to tomorrow's problems." This isn't corporate speak, it's a philosophy that prevented Lockheed from the comfortable trap of self-congratulation.

History is littered with the carcasses of companies that celebrated too long at the summit. Truly excellent leaders keep climbing while everyone else is busy taking selfies of the view.

CHARLIE MUNGER'S NEVER-ENDING QUEST

Charlie Munger never cared much for complexity.

In a world obsessed with finding the newest hack, the latest shortcut, or the most sophisticated strategy, Munger stood apart. He lived ninety-nine years, built extraordinary wealth, and influenced generations through principles so simple they fit on an index card.

I've spent years studying Munger. I want to understand how someone could maintain such clarity of thought for nearly a century.

I found three rules that formed the backbone of his approach to life.

Rule #1: Continuous Learning

"In my whole life, I have known no wise people who didn't read all the time. None, zero," Munger once said.

This was a fundamental belief that shaped his daily habits.

While his peers gradually retired from intellectual life, Munger kept a reading schedule that would exhaust someone a quarter his age. His children tell stories of finding him at three in the morning, completely absorbed in a biography, having lost all track of time.

The power in Munger's approach wasn't just that he read, but *how* he read. He built what he called a "latticework of mental models" from fields as diverse as psychology, history, physics, and biology. During a USC Law School commencement address, he put it plainly: "Develop into a lifelong self-learner through voracious reading; cultivate curiosity and strive to become a little wiser every day."

Munger never stopped actively learning. At ninety-five, he was still consuming books at a rapid pace. When others saw a man too old to learn new tricks, Munger saw each day as another opportunity to become "less stupid than yesterday."

Rule #2: Learn from Mistakes, Especially Others'

Munger had a refreshing perspective on failure. "There's no way that you can live an adequate life without making many mistakes," he often said. But he quickly followed with the crucial distinction: "It doesn't matter if you make occasional mistakes. What does matter is that you learn from them and don't make the same mistake again."

Where Munger separated himself from conventional wisdom was his insistence that the truly wise learn more from others' mistakes than their own.

"It's remarkable how much long-term advantage people like us have gotten by trying to be consistently not stupid, instead of trying to be very intelligent," he explained in a 2013 interview.

In the early 1960s, when many of his peers got into speculative ventures, Munger stepped back and studied historical market bubbles. He observed what happened to those who employed similar strategies in the past. While his peers mocked his caution, many later faced financial ruin during market corrections, while Munger remained secure.

One of Charlie's qualities I most admire was his willingness to discuss his own failures openly. Rather than hiding missteps, he frequently talked about them in speeches as "shining examples of the kind of mistake to avoid." In this way, he turned personal failures into public lessons. And that's a rare form of generosity.

Rule #3: Know Your Circle of Competence

"Knowing what you don't know is more useful than being brilliant," Munger frequently advised. In a culture that celebrates expertise, Munger's approach feels almost radical: Know the boundaries of your knowledge and respect them religiously. When everyone around him was claiming mastery in emerging fields, Munger had the confidence to say, "I don't understand this well enough to participate."

This discipline saved him countless times throughout his long career. While others ventured into territories they barely comprehended, Charlie stayed within the areas he thoroughly understood.

During a private dinner in 2010, when asked what differentiated successful people from unsuccessful ones, Munger replied, "The successful ones know the perimeter of their playground very, very well."

This means recognizing the difference between what you've studied deeply and what you've merely skimmed. It means having the humility to say, "I don't know" more often than feels comfortable.

THE SIMPLE THINGS ARE THE HARDEST

What strikes me most about Munger's rules is their simplicity. Read constantly. Learn from mistakes (especially others'). Know what you don't know.

These principles aren't complicated. They require no special intelligence or privileged background. They cost almost nothing to implement.

Yet they remain rare in practice.

Maybe that's because the simplest advice is often the hardest to follow consistently. It lacks the novelty that human brains crave. It demands patience in an impatient world. It promises no overnight transformation.

As Munger himself would say with plainspoken clarity, "Take a simple idea and take it seriously."

And that's the challenge and the opportunity. The principles that guided one of history's most impactful lives aren't locked behind some barrier we can't get through. They're available to anyone willing to take simple ideas seriously, day after day, year after year. That was Munger's genius. He followed timeless wisdom with uncommon discipline.

GOAL SETTING

Challenging ideas is not limited to the outside world or other people. I want to end this chapter by talking about a way in which I've challenged my own beliefs.

I have struggled to set goals for most of my life. I've wondered for a while what they actually do for me. When I was younger, my dad had us write down big, ambitious, long-term goals. I still have some of those handwritten notes. Two of them were:

1. Earn a college scholarship for academics or athletics.
2. After college, get a job that I actually like instead of just worrying about money.

Both came true. So, here's a reasonable question: Did they happen because I wrote them down? Or because I did the work to make them a reality?

The answer is yes.

Goals work as fuel for action, but the action is what makes it happen. This is a subtle but important distinction. As I've gotten older, I've drifted away from setting outcome-based goals and focused more on the process or a system. I began saying things like, "If I focus on the process, the outcome will take care of itself." That philosophy became central to one of my previous books (written with Brook Cupps), *The Score That Matters*. This philosophy served me well, until a conversation with lacrosse legend Paul Rabil forced me to confront a truth about my own relationship with ambition. Paul talked with me about setting big, ambitious outcome-related goals, and I realized something uncomfortable: maybe I'd stopped setting big goals because I was afraid. As Paul told me, "Most people don't set goals because the act alone is both a major and personal step in the direction of commitment, and it invites hope, fear, and the possibility of regret."

That hit me hard. It's much safer to focus solely on the process. When you do that, you have complete control. You get to decide how hard you work, how early you wake up, how dedicated you remain. But outcomes? Those involve the chaotic outside world, luck, timing, and a thousand variables you can't control. And I like being in control. Here's what I've come to realize: focusing only on the process might be a sophisticated form of self-protection. It's rational. It's smart. But it might also be limiting. The most powerful human achievements often begin with someone setting an outlandish goal that makes them and everyone else uncomfortable. Not because the goal itself creates success, but because it forces a level of commitment that wouldn't exist otherwise.

While I still believe deeply in the power of process, I think I might be limiting myself by avoiding outcome goals. By shying away from declaring what I really want to achieve, I'm protecting myself from potential disappointment but also capping my potential. What's the harm in setting a massive outcome-related goal? I don't hit it? Life goes on. But the attempt itself might take me places I'd never go otherwise. Maybe the wisest approach isn't choosing *between* process and outcomes but *understanding how they work together.* The big goals give us direction and force commitment; the process gives us the daily path forward. Neither works well without the other.

I want to challenge you to examine your own relationship with goal setting. Are you, like I was, hiding behind the safety of process-only thinking? Are there big things you've been afraid to name because it feels too vulnerable?

First, get honest about what you're avoiding. What goal would fundamentally change your life if you achieved it? What do you want so badly that you're afraid to admit? Write it down. Don't edit it. Don't make it realistic. Just write the truth.

Second, notice your resistance. Pay attention to the voice that explains why it's impossible or impractical. That voice isn't protecting you. It's limiting you. Acknowledge it and set it aside.

Third, share your goal with someone you trust. Speaking it aloud transforms it from private fantasy into something real and accountable. Choose someone who will support your ambition rather than talk you out of it.

Next, take action toward that goal this week. It doesn't have to be big, but it needs to be something you wouldn't have done while playing it safe. For instance, if your goal is to start a side business, reach out to three potential clients this week, or if you want to switch careers, schedule informational interviews with people in your target field. This creates momentum and proves you're serious.

The most impactful leaders are willing to set big, ambitious goals. They learned to live in the tension between what they want and where they are, using that gap as fuel instead of letting it paralyze them. Process versus outcome isn't really a choice. It's understanding how they work together. What goal have you been afraid to set? What would you attempt if failure weren't permanent? The answer might reveal exactly what you need to pursue.

REFLECTION QUESTIONS

- What's one "truth" that everyone in your field accepts without question, and how could you test whether it's actually true?
- When was the last time you spoke up about something you knew was wrong, and what held you back from doing it sooner?
- What complex problem are you currently facing that you could reduce to one essential action you could take today?

- What's one uncomfortable outcome goal that scares you enough that you've been avoiding writing it down?
- Looking at your recent successes, how quickly did you move from celebrating to working on what's next? Are you too comfortable with your achievements?

Take Action

- **Count everything for one week.** Pick something in your daily routine and measure it obsessively. Steps, questions asked, interruptions, time spent on tasks. Katherine Johnson counted everything, and it built the foundation for mathematical excellence. Small measurement habits compound into big advantages.
- **Simplify one complex problem to its essence.** Take something you're struggling with and reduce it to a single action you can take today. When complexity rises, the answer is to subtract until you find what's essential.
- **Set one uncomfortable outcome-based goal.** Write down something you want to achieve that scares you a little. Most people avoid big goals because they invite the possibility of failure. But the attempt itself will take you places you'd never go otherwise.
- **Read outside your field for thirty minutes daily.** Pick up books about history, science, psychology, or any area unrelated to your work. Great insights come from connecting ideas across different domains, but you can't connect what you don't know.
- **Practice saying "I don't know" more often.** When you reach the edge of your expertise, admit it. Charlie Munger built an extraordinary life by knowing the boundaries of his knowledge, respecting them, and striving to learn.
- **Study one major failure in your industry.** Look at a company or leader who fell from the top and figure out what went wrong. Learning from others' mistakes is cheaper than making them yourself, and most failures follow patterns.

- **Stop celebrating wins so quickly.** The next time you achieve something significant, acknowledge it, then start working on what's next. Perpetual dissatisfaction with the current state is what separates the excellent from the good. If you're reading a book like this, you probably already do this to some extent. (I still have a bottle of champagne in my cabinet that my literary agent gave me for writing my first book. I submitted that manuscript in 2019.)

PART II

WORK

4

The Hard Way

What Everyone Gets Wrong About Strength

Most of us get stuck because we look at the entire journey instead of the next step.

One of my favorite books is called *Bird by Bird*. In it, the author Anne Lamott tells a story about her brother when he was ten years old. He had a school report on birds due the next day that he'd put off for months. Their dad found him at the kitchen table, surrounded by unopened books, blank paper, and near tears from the overwhelming work ahead. His dad sat down beside him, put his arm around his shoulder and said, *"Bird by bird, buddy. Just take it bird by bird."*

We all do this. We look at the entire novel we want to write, the business we want to build, the retirement we want to save for, or the weight we want to lose. The gap between here and there feels impossibly wide. What happens next is predictable. We freeze. We procrastinate. We look for shortcuts that don't exist.

Anthony Consigli (CEO of Consigli Construction) told me a story about hiking a 10,000-footer in Colorado. He went with his brother, son, and a few friends, guided by an older local who looked like he lived life on his own unhurried terms. Before they started, Anthony asked the guide for a trail map. "Don't have one," the guide said. Anthony was concerned. "How do you know how to get to the top?" He pointed up and said, *"It's right up there. We just need to keep going up."*

That's it. Just keep going up. When they reached the summit, Anthony realized it was a perfect analogy for his construction business and, really, any meaningful endeavor in life. *"We just needed to keep taking one more step up."*

This is how everything significant gets accomplished.

Writing a book isn't about writing a book. It's about writing a sentence, then a paragraph. Then a page. Then doing it again tomorrow. And the next day. Raising good kids is about handling today's tantrum with patience. It's helping with tonight's homework with encouragement. It's having one good conversation at a time. Building a business is about finding one customer, solving one problem, hiring one good person, then doing it again. This applies to virtually everything meaningful, from relationships to careers to personal growth. The people who succeed aren't necessarily more talented, more intelligent, or luckier. They're often just better at taking the next step, consistently and without much fuss. The most important skill might be the ability to break down intimidating challenges into mundane tasks.

Bird by bird. Step by step. Keep going up.

The gap between average and exceptional is narrower than it seems. It's often just a willingness to take the simple next step when others become overwhelmed by the entire journey.

THE MAGIC OF HARD THINGS

The idea that "I can do hard things" transfers to everything else in life. When you push through the wall in a marathon, you're teaching yourself that barriers can be broken. And that lesson sticks with you when facing a difficult project at work or a personal setback.

Psychologists call this self-efficacy: the belief that you can execute the behaviors needed to produce specific outcomes. It's the confidence that comes from knowing firsthand that improvement is always possible, because you've done it before. You've created evidence for yourself. This confidence is context-agnostic. The marathoner doesn't just think they can run faster; they believe they can learn Chinese, start a business, or navigate a crisis. The mental framework of *better is possible* becomes the default setting.

When I talk with impactful leaders from a wide variety of industries, this trait shows up constantly. They've overcome something difficult in their past, often unrelated to their current field, and that experience became a source of strength and confidence they tap into repeatedly.

Smart organizations look beyond the résumé. They hunt for people who've faced real challenges and pushed through them in any domain. That's why good interview questions often probe for stories of difficulty. They're not trying to make you feel bad . . . They want to see how you responded to tough moments. How did you persist? Adapt? Learn something fundamental?

Companies know that technical skills can be taught. But that intrinsic quality, the quiet confidence that comes from having faced obstacles before, is what truly matters when projects go sideways. Someone who has climbed back from setbacks brings a certain resilience to the team. They don't panic at the first sign of trouble. They've developed an internal compass that says, "I've been in tough spots before. I'll find a way through this one, too."

WHY WE NEED FRICTION

Academy Award–winning screenwriter and director Aaron Sorkin once said he "worships at the altar of intention and obstacle." This is a window into how stories work, and maybe how life works, too. Every good story has a similar framework: someone wants something, something stops them from getting it. They fight through the challenge and eventually get it. That's it. The magic happens in the space between the initial desire and the earning of the thing. Sorkin calls this worship because he understands the obstacle is the best friend the story ever had. Think about the stories you remember most. They're never about people who got what they wanted easily. They're about the ones who had to fight for it, sacrifice, or improve themselves to get it.

The obstacle does something beautiful. It reveals who the character really is. When everything is going well, we all look the same. When things get hard, our true nature emerges. This is why Sorkin's characters are so compelling. They don't just deal with external problems. They face moral dilemmas that force them to choose between living up to their values or not. The best obstacles make characters question their entire worldview. There's an economic principle at work here. Scarcity creates value. Easy victories feel cheap. Hard-won conquests are meaningful. When a character struggles against real obstacles, the audience invests emotionally. We root for them because success isn't guaranteed. The harder the path, the more we care about the destination.

This worship of intention and obstacle reflects something deeper about human nature. We're wired to care about struggle. We respect people who overcome adversity more than people who never faced it. Sorkin understands that his characters need to earn their victories. That's how real transformation works. Nobody changes when life is easy. We change when it's hard. The obstacle isn't something to overcome quickly so you can get to the good stuff. *The obstacle is the good stuff.*

ALCHEMY OF ADVERSITY

We love stories of people succeeding despite the odds. But what if it's not despite but because of them? A good example is Michael Jordan's "Flu Game" in the 1997 NBA Finals. Jordan, battling what was likely food poisoning (though called the flu at the time), could barely get back to the bench during timeouts without the help of Scottie Pippen holding him up. He was dehydrated and exhausted. Yet he scored 38 points, including the decisive bucket that gave the Bulls a 3–2 series lead.

What's fascinating isn't just that Jordan played while sick, it's that he took it up another level (even for him) while under the weather. This paradox exists everywhere if you look for it.

My daughter Charlie (yes, I'm about to compare my daughter to the greatest basketball player of all time; this is what dads do) recently played against a much bigger and older team in a soccer tournament. I watched from the sidelines as she took a hard hit from one of their defenders and went down. She got up limping, fighting back tears, visibly mad and hurt. Within the next few minutes, still hobbling at three-quarters speed, she got a beautiful cross from a teammate and buried it in the back of the net. Her best play came immediately after her worst moment.

At the 1996 Olympics, despite a severely injured ankle, Kerry Strug executed a near-perfect vault to earn America's first team gold in women's gymnastics. The image of her landing on one foot before collapsing in pain became iconic. Tiger Woods won the 2008 U.S. Open while playing with a double stress fracture in his left tibia and a torn ACL. Doctors later said they were shocked he could even walk, let alone compete. Ernest Hemingway wrote his most enduring works while battling depression. Abraham Lincoln led America through its darkest hour while fighting his own melancholy. Beethoven composed his Ninth Symphony while almost entirely deaf. Serena Williams won the 2017 Australian Open while eight weeks pregnant, battling morning sickness and hormonal changes that would sideline most non-athletes entirely. What explains this pattern? Several mechanisms seem to be at work.

1. The Biological Override

When we face physical or emotional threats, our bodies activate the sympathetic nervous system, what we call the *fight-or-flight* response. Adrenaline, norepinephrine, and cortisol flood the bloodstream. Heart rate increases. Blood diverts to major muscle groups. This response evolved over millions of years for survival, but in competitive contexts, it functions as a performance enhancer. Pain receptors temporarily dampen. Glucose releases for immediate energy. Your mind sharpens.

2. The Laser-Focus Effect

The human mind typically juggles dozens of thoughts simultaneously. We worry about past mistakes and future outcomes. We think about how we look, what others think, what we'll do later.

Pain cuts through this noise like nothing else.

When you're hurting or facing significant adversity, the mind's bandwidth narrows dramatically. Sports psychologists refer to this as "perceptual narrowing" or "attentional focusing," a survival mechanism that forces concentration on immediate threats and opportunities while filtering out peripheral information. For Jordan, the complexity of basketball was momentarily simplified. The crowded arena, the championship pressure, and the media scrutiny all faded against his body's singular demand to perform this specific task before collapsing. For Charlie, distractions, like the embarrassment of being knocked down, the intimidation of larger opponents, and worries about technique, vanished. There was only the ball, the goal, and the direct path between them.

3. Liberation from Expectations

Performance anxiety typically stems from our expectations and those of others. The fear of failing to meet these standards creates what psychologists call "explicit monitoring," where we overthink automatic processes. This explains why basketball players sometimes miss free throws in crucial moments, or why experienced public speakers suddenly forget their words. But when we're sick or injured? Expectations drop dramatically. The narrative changes from "I must succeed" to "I'm just trying to survive." Paradoxically, this releases us from the very pressure that inhibits peak performance.

4. The Defiance Dividend

There's something uniquely motivating about proving others wrong or proving something to ourselves. Adversity triggers a psychological response that taps into our deeper competitive nature. We see this in data from endurance sports. Researchers analyzing marathon finishing times found that runners push hardest when approaching round numbers. The difference between 4:01 and 3:59 is a couple seconds. But psychologically? It's everything. That barrier becomes personal. When Charlie got knocked down, her anger and determination to prove herself became emotional rocket fuel. When she got back up, it was a lot more than just scoring a goal. It was more about proving to herself that she's tough and resilient.

■ ■ ■

What makes these stories so compelling is the glimpse they provide into our untapped capacity. They suggest that our normal performance operates well below our actual capabilities and that we possess reserves we access only under extraordinary circumstances. Exercise physiologist Timothy Noakes proposed the influential Central Governor Theory in the 1990s. The theory suggests our brains actively regulate physical exertion to prevent catastrophic physiological failure. According to Noakes, these neural limiters aren't fixed; they can adjust based on emotional states, perceived importance of the task, and competitive environments. While not universally accepted in exercise science, the theory helps explain why we sometimes access seemingly impossible performance reserves during moments of crisis or intense competition. This explains documented cases of seemingly impossible feats: parents lifting cars off trapped children or soldiers continuing to fight despite severe injuries.

The most practical application might be recognizing that our perceived limitations often have more headroom than we realize. We might benefit from occasionally simulating the mental states that illness or injuries produce. Elite military units train in extreme discomfort to develop this capacity. Some creative professionals intentionally work under artificial constraints or deadlines to mimic the focusing effects of genuine pressure.

The next time you face adversity before an important task, consider that it might be a catalyst for your performance.

WHEN CONDITIONS AREN'T IDEAL

Katie Knight does hard things, like ultramarathons and Tough Mudder championships. In an interview with

Cameron Hanes, she talks about her approach in a way that struck me. It's what I think a Learning Leader mentality looks like:

> No one cares what you can do fresh. Anybody, when they're fresh, physically or mentally, can do a lot. It's when you get past that point where . . . the body starts to get fatigued; your mind starts to feel weak, that's when it matters.

The core truth Knight is highlighting is that genuine capability is measured when conditions are far from ideal. This applies broadly across many domains: In professional life, anyone can perform well when they're well-rested. The problems are straightforward, and there's no pressure. But real professional value shows up when:

- You're in month six of a challenging project and facing unexpected obstacles.
- You need to maintain quality work during a personal crisis.
- You have to make clear decisions at the end of a twelve-hour day.
- Multiple deadlines converge, and you need to stay focused despite the stress.

In leadership, it's similar. Many can lead effectively when the team is harmonious, and goals are being met. It's easy to be the team captain when you're winning by 40. But true leadership emerges during:

- Times of organizational uncertainty or change

- When team morale is low, and you need to rebuild motivation
- After setbacks, when the easy path would be to give up
- When you have to make unpopular but necessary decisions

The quality Knight is really talking about is mental stamina. The ability to maintain high standards and clear thinking even when fatigue, stress, or adversity would give you an easy excuse to lower them. This is what separates consistent high performers from those who can only excel under ideal conditions.

It's a harsh truth that applies far beyond sports. What you can do when everything isn't going according to plan is what sets you apart. This seems backward because most spend their time practicing under ideal conditions. But life has a funny way of testing you when conditions are anything but ideal. We avoid difficulty in practice because we think it will help us perform better. But that's like trying to learn to swim in a kiddie pool and expecting to handle the ocean.

The people who thrive are the ones who have figured out how to function when things go wrong. And things always go wrong. This connects to a bigger idea about getting stronger from setbacks rather than just surviving them. Part of *the price of becoming* someone who makes a real difference is learning to build strength from the very things that break other people down.

The person who stays calm and effective when exhausted or under pressure isn't just performing well in the moment. They're developing a deeper capacity for whatever comes next. Because there's always a next challenge waiting.

This is about understanding that fatigue and difficulty aren't obstacles to performance; they're the arena where real performance happens. Most people intuitively know this. But they still spend 90 percent of their preparation time working under perfect conditions. Then they're surprised when real challenges feel overwhelming. The solution isn't to make yourself miserable. It's to gradually expand your comfort zone by deliberately practicing under less-than-ideal conditions. Start small but start somewhere. The world doesn't care what you can do on your best day. It cares about what you can do when it's hard. When the PowerPoint doesn't show up on the screen, and you have a room full of people waiting to hear you present. It's when your colleague doesn't do their part of the project, and you have to be ready to fill in and make it look seamless. The person who does the extra work, the one who overprepares, the one who *has a plan, works the plan, and* ***plans for the unexpected*** is the one who has the best chance for excellence.

And that's actually good news. Because while talent is unevenly distributed, resilience can be built. It just requires accepting that the hard part isn't an exception to prepare for, it's the whole point.

THE BEST KIND OF HARD

The trail was steep, the weather questionable, and about halfway up, bestselling author and endurance runner Alex Hutchinson's daughter asked, "Dad, are we going to make it?" He said he didn't know. And that was the point. There's something fascinating about how we're drawn to uncertainty, even as we spend most of our lives trying to eliminate it. The most valuable experiences often come wrapped in a layer of "maybe," maybe we can do it, maybe we'll fail, maybe we'll surprise ourselves.

When Alex recounted that moment on *The Learning Leader Show* with me, he said, *"We are wired to explore. We're wired to push our limits."* And here's the key part: *"If you know before you start a challenge that you're going to complete it, that challenge loses all of its meaning and interest."*

Think about how much we pay for uncertainty. The global sports industry is worth hundreds of billions of dollars, built entirely on people's willingness to watch games whose outcomes they don't know. We get mad when someone spoils a movie ending because they've stolen something valuable from us, the gift of not knowing what comes next.

I've been thinking about this lately in the context of achievement and satisfaction. There's a version of success that comes from checking predetermined boxes, the kind where you know exactly what you need to do and exactly what you'll get if you do it. Then there's the kind that comes from venturing into territory where the outcome isn't guaranteed. The first kind pays the bills. The second kind changes who you are.

When Hutchinson and his wife take their daughters hiking, they're learning something more valuable than outdoor skills. They're developing a relationship with uncertainty that will serve them better than any predetermined path could. That feeling of "I can do anything" they get at the summit isn't just about the hike, it's about proving to themselves that they can handle not knowing.

This mirrors something I've noticed studying excellent

leaders across different fields: They're good at doing hard things where a lot of uncertainty exists.

Think of any meaningful achievement in your life. Its significance likely stems from the moments of doubt, the internal struggles, and the real possibility of failure that accompanied it. This is why artificial challenges often feel hollow; our psyche recognizes the difference between genuine uncertainty and manufactured obstacles.

The irony is rich: We spend a ton of energy trying to make outcomes more certain, only to pay a premium for experiences defined by their uncertainty. Maybe that's not a contradiction at all. Maybe it's just human nature acknowledging what we deeply know: the best kind of hard isn't knowing you'll get there, it's not knowing and going anyway.

THE HIDDEN BENEFITS OF HUNGER

Scientific research supports the connection between "hunger" (both metaphorical and literal) and achievement.

The "Need for Achievement" theory developed by psychologist David McClelland, showed that individuals with a high need for achievement tend to:

- Set challenging goals
- Take calculated risks
- Seek feedback
- Take personal responsibility for their performance

Here's what's wild about how our brains work: hunger actually makes us smarter. Not just food hunger, but any kind of wanting something we don't have. When you're hungry for anything, your brain floods with dopamine, and suddenly you're more focused and motivated than you were five minutes ago.

A 2019 study in *Nature Communications* proved something most of us suspected but couldn't explain. Moderate stress and hunger don't hurt your thinking. They improve it. Your brain doesn't want comfort when it needs to solve problems. It wants a little tension.

But how does this actually work in your body? A hormone called ghrelin is doing most of the heavy lifting. This was traditionally just thought of as a hunger hormone that makes you want to eat. But newer research has shown it actually enhances memory formation and learning. This might explain why being moderately hungry can make us more alert and focused. It's an evolutionary adaptation that helped our ancestors stay sharp when they needed to find food.

HISTORICAL-SOCIOLOGICAL RESEARCH: THE "IMMIGRANT EFFECT"

Research by multiple economists has shown that immigrants, often driven by necessity and a hunger for success, are:

- Twice as likely to start businesses
- More likely to file patents
- More likely to pursue higher education

The critical finding across all these studies is that moderate levels of "hunger," whether it's for achievement, recognition, or improvement, tend to optimize human performance. It's about finding the sweet spot where the drive pushes you to excel without pushing you over the edge. The research suggests that being "hungry" isn't just a motivational metaphor, it's deeply rooted in our biology, psychology, and social structures as a catalyst for achievement and innovation. The key is harnessing this drive in a sustainable and productive way.

Soichiro Honda's story is a great example of relentless willingness to get after it. In his early years, Honda worked as an apprentice in an auto repair shop in Tokyo, often sleeping in the shop to save money and spending every free moment learning about engines. He was so obsessed with understanding mechanics that he would take engines apart just to see how they worked, often staying up all night reassembling them.

One of the most telling stories about his appetite for excellence came after multiple failures. In 1938, he founded a company to make piston rings for Toyota. He was so determined to get the contract that he pawned his wife's jewelry to help fund the venture. But his first batches were rejected because they didn't meet Toyota's quality standards. Instead of quitting, Honda enrolled in engineering classes and spent endless nights experimenting with different materials and techniques. Completely absorbed in his work, he would often forget to eat. He lived in his workshop, sleeping just a few hours a night, driven by an obsessive desire to solve the problem. After World War II, Japan faced severe fuel shortages. Honda saw an opportunity where others saw crisis. He began collecting surplus generator engines from the military, attaching them to bicycles to create makeshift motorcycles. When he ran out of engines, he started making his own. His workshop was initially so small that he could barely turn around in it, but his hunger for innovation never diminished. I love how he responded to failure . . . When asked about his numerous crashes, failed prototypes, and business setbacks, he famously said, *"Success represents the 1% of your work which results from the 99% that is called failure."* He viewed each setback as valuable data for his next attempt.

Honda's hunger was an almost spiritual devotion to the pursuit of technical excellence. Even after his company became successful, he never lost this drive. He would still regularly visit factory floors well into his later years, getting his hands dirty and challenging engineers to push boundaries. His story resonates because his hunger was about creation and innovation. He wasn't satisfied with making something good; he wanted to make something better than had ever existed before. This kind of hunger drove him to transform a bombed-out post-war workshop into one of the world's most innovative companies.

DO THE HARD

In 1952, Edmund Hillary failed to reach the summit of Mount Everest. He returned a year later and succeeded where he previously failed. At a dinner honoring his achievement, Hillary stood up and addressed the mountain directly through a nearby window: *"You defeated me once. You won't defeat me again."* This is the cool realization about hard things: it's what happens inside your brain when you refuse to stay defeated.

I've been curious about this pattern for years. When you voluntarily do hard things, you get something beyond the immediate result. You gain a sort of confidence that works like compound interest for the rest of your life.

Scott Belsky said it on *The Learning Leader Show*: *"Overcoming personal challenges develops self-efficacy, a form of transferable confidence."* This explains why certain people seem to excel at whatever they touch. When you push through the discomfort of a challenging pursuit, your brain literally rewires its understanding of what's possible. As Belsky points out, "You're proving to yourself that 'a faster time' or 'a better quarter' (whatever the challenge) is always possible."

The interesting part is how this confidence jumps categories. It becomes context agnostic. It's a portable skill.

This happened to Warren Buffett. He was scared of public speaking early in his career. It physically made him sick. But he forced himself to teach night classes at the University of Nebraska. The discomfort was extreme, but he pushed through it. Years later, he became known for his ability to explain complex financial concepts to shareholders. That initial struggle with public speaking built confidence that transferred to other communication challenges throughout his career. This explains why smart employers look for evidence of overcoming challenges when hiring. They understand what Belsky describes as "this strong sense of transferrable self-efficacy," which manifests as resilience across domains. The equation might look like:

Difficulty × Persistence = Transferable Confidence

Most people try to avoid difficulty. They stick to what feels comfortable. This makes sense in the short term. Why suffer if you don't have to? But the long-term math works differently. The temporary pain of doing hard things pays dividends across your entire life. The person who voluntarily embraces difficulty builds an asset that others can't buy: the unshakable knowledge that they can handle whatever comes next. So do hard things. They transform who you become for all the moments that follow.

DA VINCI'S RIGOR

If you open Leonardo da Vinci's notebooks, you'll find a phrase scattered throughout the thousands of pages: *ostinato rigore. Persistent rigor.* Relentless precision. Stubborn thoroughness.

Most interpret this as da Vinci's personal motto. Historians will tell you he never formally claimed it. Doesn't matter. The phrase captures what separated da Vinci from everyone else around him. Look at the *Mona Lisa.* Started around 1503, da Vinci worked on this single painting for over fifteen years, until his death in 1519. Giorgio Vasari, a contemporary biographer, described how da Vinci would sometimes spend an entire day just observing the painting, add a single brushstroke, and consider it a day's work. His peers thought this was madness. But da Vinci understood something fundamental about excellence: *greatness lives in the microscopic details others are unwilling to pursue.*

This was his standard operating procedure. When da Vinci studied human anatomy, he created over 240 detailed drawings based on actual dissections. While other artists learned just enough anatomy to make their figures look right, da Vinci mapped entire vascular systems, documented muscle attachments, and measured proportional relationships with scientific precision. Most stop at "good enough." Da Vinci didn't.

In 1503, when commissioned to divert the Arno River, da Vinci produced topographical maps so accurate they astonished modern historians. He calculated water volumes and flow rates with painstaking detail. Historian Carlo Pedretti later called it "the most thorough study of a river conducted up to that time." Da Vinci was redefining what the job could be. His bird flight studies reveal the same pattern. Hundreds of detailed observations about wing movements, air resistance, and balance fill his notebooks. "The bird is an instrument working according to mathematical law," he wrote, followed by calculations that wouldn't be fully understood until centuries later when modern aerodynamics emerged.

What's particularly revealing is that da Vinci pursued this level of excellence largely for himself. Many of his most thorough studies remained hidden in private notebooks. His commitment to understanding wasn't performance art for others; *it was his internal standard.* Francesco Melzi, da Vinci's assistant who inherited these notebooks, described how his mentor would revisit ideas repeatedly, refining them until he had explored every aspect of a problem. Da Vinci's few students often complained about his methods, finding them frustratingly slow. He would insist they master fundamental techniques through endless repetition before advancing. This commitment came with trade-offs. Da Vinci completed remarkably few paintings compared to other artists, like Raphael. Yet his works have endured for 500 years, while thousands of "more efficient" creations from the same era have been forgotten. Most people never reach excellence because they're unwilling to tolerate the thousands of tiny iterations required to get there. They want the outcome without the process. Da Vinci's life demonstrates that genius isn't a moment of inspiration; it's a lifetime of attention to details others ignore.

THE 54 PERCENT RULE

Even da Vinci's level of rigor doesn't guarantee constant victory. Roger Federer won 103 singles titles. He won 20 Grand Slams. He was ranked number one in the world for 237 consecutive weeks. By any measure, he's one of the greatest tennis players who ever lived.

In a 2024 commencement speech, Federer asked the graduates a question: "What percentage of points do you think I won throughout my career?"

"Only 54 percent." Think about that. One of the most dominant athletes in history lost 46 percent of the points he played. Nearly half. And that was enough to make him great. "Whatever game you play in life, you're going to lose. A point, a match, a season, a job. You want to become a master at overcoming hard moments. That is the sign of a champion."

The best in the world are the best because they know they'll lose sometimes, and they understand it's all about how they *choose* to respond. Da Vinci's rigor didn't eliminate failure. Federer's talent didn't prevent losing. The commitment to bouncing back is what separates them from everyone else.

BRUTAL TRUTH ABOUT ENTITLEMENT

My first two years in college killed a belief I'd carried my entire life: that hard work entitled me to results.

It doesn't. The world doesn't care about how hard you think you worked. It cares about the value you create for others.

The day after graduating from Centerville High School, I moved to Oxford, Ohio, to show my future teammates at Miami University that I was willing to go to the early-morning workouts, learn all their names, keep my mouth shut, and work. Over the next two years, through countless practices, weight-room time, extra film sessions, and meetings with coaches, I tried to do all of the extra work needed for a quarterback to earn the starting job and help the team win.

Fast-forward to the second game of my sophomore season. We're at the University of Iowa playing a tough and physical Hawkeye team. Ben Roethlisberger (the other quarterback) and I are both playing in the game (rotating at QB and receiver) and throughout the game, we were getting hit hard. Coach Terry Hoeppner walked up to us on the sideline in between an offensive series and said, *"That's it! Ben, you're in. Ryan you're only playing if he gets hurt. We can't afford to lose you both."*

After the game we had a meeting, and Coach Hoeppner confirmed his earlier decision that I would be the backup quarterback moving forward. I was devastated. I felt as if I had earned the job through my work from the two previous years. But I was wrong. *"Ryan . . . Ben gives us a better chance to win than you do. We're going with him."* It was that simple. And that hard.

This is how the world actually works. Companies don't succeed because their founders work hard, they win because they solve problems customers care about. Investors don't make money because they study more than others, they make money because they make good decisions that compound over time. The gap between effort and reward is one of the hardest pills to swallow in life. We love stories about hustle and grit because they make success feel controllable. But the world is more ruthless than that. It rewards value creation, which doesn't always relate to how many hours you put in or how much you think you deserve it. This doesn't mean you shouldn't work hard. The lesson wasn't that effort doesn't matter. It's that effort must translate into value for others.

When we believe we deserve something like a job, recognition, or wealth, we focus on what we're owed rather than what we can offer. I've found that the moment you let go of entitlement and focus purely on creating value for others, opportunities multiply. It's counterintuitive: the less you feel the world owes you, the more the world tends to give you. But you have to be willing to earn it every single day.

Professor Adam Grant has seen this become a troubling trend with his students at the University of Pennsylvania. *"They're saying 'My grade doesn't reflect the effort I put into the course.' Public service announcement: You don't get an A for effort. You earn it for excellence. Success is measured by the level of mastery you show, not how hard you work."*

I DIDN'T JUST DABBLE

At my 2025 Learning Leader Growth Summit in Scottsdale, I hosted Ed Latimore, heavyweight boxer, physics graduate, competitive chess player, and bestselling author, for a surprise live podcast. As we talked, Ed shared thoughts that resonated deeply with everyone in the room.

One phrase particularly hit me. Ed mentioned wanting to *"beef up his obituary."* It was a powerful way to frame a life well-lived, not as a collection of accolades, but as a story worth telling. Near the end of our talk, I asked Ed what exactly he wanted to do to beef up his obituary, and what he hoped would be written in it someday. He paused, the room falling silent in anticipation. Then, with quiet conviction, he simply said: *"I didn't just dabble."*

Those four words reveal something important about how we should think about our time here. A lot of people like to keep their options open, try different things, maintain flexibility. This sounds smart. But there's a hidden price to dabbling that compounds over time: the opportunity cost of depth. True freedom often comes from commitment, not optionality. When you commit fully to something, you unlock levels of mastery and satisfaction unavailable to dabblers. You gain the freedom that comes with expertise.

Ed gets this. He wasn't suggesting we need grand achievements or public recognition. He was making a more subtle point about engagement. About showing up completely for the things and people that matter. About creating value that outlasts us. I think about this a lot now. We live in an era overflowing with options, which makes it the golden age of dabbling. Social media shows us a thousand lives we could be living instead of the one we are. Jim Collins talked with me about this problem on *The Learning Leader Show*, and found something counterintuitive: the best companies weren't the ones with the most options or the slickest strategies. They were hedgehogs. They found one thing they could be the best in the world at, something they were deeply passionate about, something that drove their economic engine, and they stuck with it relentlessly. While foxes knew many things, hedgehogs knew one big thing. The hedgehogs won.

When I look back at my own life someday, I hope the evidence shows that I understood what matters. That I committed fully to being a good husband, dad, and friend. That I did work worth doing and did it well. That I created more value than I captured. In other words, I hope they'll say I didn't just dabble.

REFLECTION QUESTIONS

- What intimidating goal have you been avoiding because you're looking at the entire journey instead of just the next step you could take today?
- Think about the hardest thing you've ever accomplished. How has that experience given you confidence in completely unrelated areas of your life?
- When you face a challenging situation, do you typically look for ways to make it easier, or do you see the difficulty itself as valuable training?
- What's one area where you currently perform well under ideal conditions but haven't tested yourself when things get messy or stressful?
- Looking at your recent achievements, how much of your satisfaction came from the outcome versus the uncertainty and struggle of getting there?
- What story are you telling yourself about what you "deserve" that might be preventing you from focusing on the value you actually create?
- When was the last time you voluntarily chose to do something difficult with no guarantee of success, and what did that teach you about your capabilities?

Take Action

- **Break one large project into daily actions.** Pick something that feels really big and identify the smallest possible step you can take today. Then take it. Tomorrow, take the next smallest step. You climb the mountain one step at a time.

- **Practice under poor conditions.** The next time you rehearse a presentation, practice with distractions (do it without the PowerPoint presentation or rehearse with a colleague who is looking at their phone disinterested or interrupts you while presenting). When you train for something physical, do it when you're already tired or when it's hot and humid. Most people only practice under perfect conditions, then wonder why they struggle when life gets messy.

- **Choose one uncomfortable challenge this month.** Sign up to do something that scares you a little. A race you're not sure you can finish, a conversation you've been avoiding, a skill you've never tried (improv class, guitar lessons, learn a second language). Your brain needs evidence that you can handle uncertainty.

- **Track your performance when things go wrong.** Notice how you respond when you're tired, stressed, or facing setbacks. Most people's true capabilities only show up when conditions are far from ideal.

- **Embrace the suck for thirty days.** Pick one area where you've been avoiding difficulty and lean into it. Cold showers, difficult conversations, learning a hard skill. The specific challenge matters less than proving to yourself that you can handle discomfort.

- **Question what you think you deserve.** Write down three things you believe you've earned but haven't received. Then honestly evaluate whether you've created enough value to justify those expectations.

- **Find your *ostinato rigore*.** Choose one project or skill and commit to a level of thoroughness that seems unreasonable to others. Most people stop at "good enough." Greatness lives in the details others won't pursue.

- **Document your "I can do hard things" evidence.** Keep a running list of difficult things you've accomplished. When you face new challenges, remind yourself that you have a track record of figuring things out.

- **Plan for when you want to quit.** Before starting something difficult, write down the reasons you might want to stop and your strategy for pushing through anyway. Most people quit because they haven't prepared for the moment when quitting feels logical.

5

The Long Game

Daily Inputs, Extraordinary Outputs

Growing up in Gaithersburg, Maryland, Paul Rabil was encouraged to try many different extracurricular activities, from sports like basketball and soccer to playing musical instruments. Eventually, however, Paul fell in love with the hard-hitting, high-velocity sport of lacrosse, devoting more of his time, thought, and energy to mastering the sport.

He didn't become one of the greatest lacrosse players in history because he was born the most gifted. He outperformed his competitors by making a promise to himself: *take one hundred shots a day, every day.*

This chapter is about what it means to commit to a process, breaking your long-term goals down into clear, manageable daily actions that compound over time. It's about taking full ownership of your development and refusing to leave growth to chance. When you commit to a process, you're investing in a sustained, directional effort that builds skill, self-confidence, and a sense of personal agency over time. This is about focusing on the behaviors that lead to the outcomes you want.

Lacrosse became young Paul's obsession, and that single-minded focus led him to a middle-school lacrosse camp at Loyola University. There, the players got to hear from Tony Seaman, the only coach in Division I men's lacrosse history to guide three different schools to the NCAA Tournament.

"Who here wants to play college lacrosse?" Seaman asked Paul and his fellow eighth graders. As Rabil recounted to me, every kid raised his hand. "Okay," Seaman continued. "Now, who wants to get a full scholarship to play Division I lacrosse?" All the hands stayed up. Seaman smiled: "It's a simple recipe." Everyone leaned forward in anticipation.

"From this day forward, you're going to shoot one hundred shots a day," Seaman said. "Do that, and I guarantee you; you'll get a Division I scholarship."

Paul sat back in his chair, baffled. "That's it? Thirty minutes of shooting? That can't be all there is to it."

But the shots weren't the point, Seaman explained. Consistency was: "Miss a day, and the guarantee is off the table," Seaman said. "That means you must find time to get your shots in on the net when you don't have access to a net. When you're on vacation with your family. When it's raining outside. When there's a blizzard. No excuses. Starting today, you've got to commit. You've got to find your way to a goal and get your hundred shots in *no matter what.*"

Years later, after Rabil had earned the promised full-ride lacrosse scholarship at a Division I school, he finally understood that Seaman had only made such a promise to a bunch of kid lacrosse players of varying skill levels because he knew that *anyone* who demonstrated that level of commitment to something was going to succeed. Talent is abundant; commitment is rare.

At the time, of course, middle-school Paul thought this straightforward daily ritual would be easy. It was only as the weeks passed that the realization dawned on him: "Wow," he remembers thinking, "this is a lot more difficult than I thought." But he stuck with the daily habit, and his accuracy improved. He became an elite scorer. Years later, as a pro, he even set a record for the fastest lacrosse shot: 111 miles per hour (a record that has since been broken). More importantly, Rabil saw that doing the daily grind without fail delivered compounded returns. A single movement repeated over and over, day after day, created a ripple effect, improving every aspect of his game. By boiling his growth strategy down to one non-negotiable commitment and honoring it *no matter what*, the "rest took care of itself."

For Paul Rabil, a hundred shots a day instilled discipline. They forged resilience. They built a work ethic that carried him far beyond the lacrosse field, shaping his entire approach to life and business. His story illustrates a fundamental truth that applies across disciplines: consistency leads to transformational outcomes. While it's tempting to think success lies in explosive breakthroughs or moments of genius, most often, it results from a single action repeated over time with full effort and no shortcuts. Those hundred shots are a metaphor for commitment, identity, and the long-term rewiring of your character. Who you become by keeping a promise to yourself matters far more than the individual result of any given day.

This kind of deliberate repetition also builds "self-efficacy," that deep sense of personal agency and capability we discussed in Chapter 4. When you repeatedly show up and follow through on your intentions, you reinforce a powerful internal belief: *"I am someone who honors my commitments."* Over time, this belief becomes self-fulfilling. You don't just practice discipline. You become a disciplined person. This distinction is key. Don't "fake it till you make it." Forge a new identity through effort and follow-through.

DAILY PRACTICE

This is the essence of working a process. The real reward of an intense daily practice isn't just mastery of a single skill. It's who you become in the process of committing to your routine, day after day, year after year. As Paul Rabil discovered, cultivating grit through a daily ritual doesn't just make you better at one thing. It rewires your mindset. It teaches you how to push through when you don't feel like showing up. It trains you to find a way to get the work done regardless of the obstacles. That's why after Rabil's playing career ended, the hundred-shots-a-day discipline continues to serve him.

After an illustrious collegiate career at Johns Hopkins, where Rabil won All-America honors four years in a row, led the team to two championships, and set playoff records that still stand, he went on to dominate as a professional player. But his biggest challenge was yet to come. In 2018, he co-founded the Premier Lacrosse League (PLL) with his brother, taking on the brutal realities of entrepreneurship: raising capital, winning over skeptical investors, and building a league from the ground up. All while continuing to play professionally.

Rabil quickly realized that business, like lacrosse, rewards those who show up and put in the reps, day after day. Whether he was securing funding, pitching media deals, or handling the operational chaos involved in launching a league, Rabil has relied on the same approach that shaped his playing career: consistent, focused effort over short bursts of inspiration.

Many assume that greatness is a matter of talent, that the best performers in any field are simply wired differently from the rest of us. But time and again, research and real-world examples tell a different story, that the separator isn't ability but action, repeated over and over, especially when no one is watching. For Rabil, shooting a hundred times a day wasn't glamorous. It wasn't a grand, dramatic act of willpower. He did it because he understood that consistency compounds. The willingness to show up every single day, regardless of motivation, mood, or circumstances, separates the elite from the average.

"The reason Fortune 500 companies recruit student-athletes," Rabil told me, "is that those candidates have already learned how to be a great teammate, work really hard, and develop discipline and commitment. The hundred-shots-a-day mindset translates very well into the corporate world. It also translates into relationships and personal growth."

So, what are your hundred shots? Producer, director, and screenwriter Brian Koppelman told me he's maintained a daily writing practice for over thirty years, writing three pages every morning before 7 a.m.: "The pages don't need to be good; they need to be done."

Every field has its own version of this kind of daily discipline: small, repetitive actions that, done consistently over time, create big-time results:

- For a writer, it might be five hundred words a day, no matter what. Not waiting for inspiration, not obsessing over perfection. Just getting words down. Over a year, that's 182,500 words, or three full-length books.
- For a salesperson, it might be ten outreach calls before noon. Not waiting for leads to come in, not making excuses. Just making calls. The top closers aren't always the most charismatic. They're the ones who pick up the phone.
- For an entrepreneur, it might be an hour of direct engagement with customer feedback every day. Not getting lost in the big-picture vision and staying grounded in what real customers say, even when they say they aren't happy.
- For an athlete, it might be an extra thirty minutes of skill work after practice. When the competition goes home, the elite performers choose extra work.
- For a musician, it might be playing scales or improvising for twenty minutes before diving into complex pieces. The greats don't just perform; they drill the fundamentals daily.
- For a leader, it might be one handwritten note of appreciation to a team member every day. Culture is built through small, intentional acts that reinforce values.

The specific action will look different depending on your field, but the principle remains the same: relentless consistency beats intermittent intensity.

If you're not sure where to start, here's a simple framework for identifying the right daily action and making it stick:

1. **Brainstorm every behavior tied to your goal.** Think broadly about the field or skill you want to improve. Make a list of every relevant behavior or activity, from the strategic (designing a sales pitch) to the mundane (reviewing performance notes). Don't worry about quality (yet), just get it all down.
2. **Filter for autonomy.** Now go through your list and cross out anything you can't control 100 percent. For example, you can't control whether someone buys from you, but you can control how many calls you make. Your hundred shots should be fully within your control. They're things you can do regardless of what happens around you.
3. **Choose the one behavior that matters most . . . and commit.** Ask yourself, "If I only did this one thing every single day, would it move me toward my goal?" Pick a behavior that's both meaningful and sustainable. Choose the task that will quietly compound over time.
4. **Lock it in with habits.** To make the action stick, tie it to something you already do. Set an alarm. Put a sticky note on your laptop. Stack it onto an existing habit (e.g., "After I make my coffee, I send my daily follow-ups").

The smaller the barrier to starting, the more likely you are to follow through.

5. **Get accountable.** Find a partner you trust, ideally, someone with their own hundred shots, and text each other when you've completed the day's action. The goal isn't perfection. It's momentum. One check-in becomes ten. Ten becomes a streak. The streak becomes your new baseline.

At this point, you may be wondering, when can I put down the stick and enjoy my success? The answer is never. Your hundred shots aren't just about helping you grow but also about holding on to the growth you've achieved. Recent research shows that our skills decay rapidly when we don't invest steady effort in maintaining them. Worse, we drastically underestimate how quickly our abilities fade, by as much as 60 percent, even though we're perfectly able to judge and predict skill decay in others. If you want to hold on to everything you've worked so hard to build, keep swinging that stick *every single day.*

Most people rely on motivation, which comes and goes. But those who sustain excellence build it on habits. They commit to simple, repeatable actions, small enough to do every day but meaningful enough to create exponential results over time. So, ask yourself: what's the daily commitment you can make, the non-negotiable practice that, if done consistently, will separate you from the rest? Because in the end, it's not about waiting for the perfect opportunity. It's about doing the work.

Don't quit. Almost everyone does.

TAKE *NO* OFF THE TABLE

Back at that lacrosse camp, when Coach Tony Seaman guaranteed a Division I scholarship to every kid who took a hundred shots a day, he was drawing a hard line. He didn't say, "Shoot a hundred shots a day, unless it's raining, or you're on vacation, or you're tired, or you're just not in the mood."

He said, "No excuses." Miss a day, and the guarantee is off the table.

Its simplicity made it sound easy. It wasn't. That was the point. What derails people isn't a lack of desire or ability, it's all the tiny, seemingly reasonable justifications. The excuses. Dramatic failures are rare. These subtle, socially acceptable opt-outs are what take us out of contention. They're so dangerous because they sound normal, and they are. But normal excuses produce normal results. They leave you right where you are.

The most powerful tool for personal growth is to make a promise to yourself and then follow through on it without caveats.

This is where you get real self-respect. Not from positive self-talk or affirmations but from watching yourself do what you said you'd do, especially when you don't feel like it. Doing that daily builds integrity and a sense of personal agency. You start to see yourself as someone who can be trusted with responsibilities, goals, and your future.

Don't rely on willpower. Research has found strategic intervention to be the most effective way to avoid failures of self-control when adopting new behaviors. That means thinking ahead about smoothing the way. When I write in the morning, I do it the same way every time. I wake up early before the world can interrupt me. No phone, email, or other excuse-generators. I get some water and go to work. Kill excuses before you can make them.

It's about removing optionality. You don't ask yourself if you feel like doing it. You just do it. Take debate, deliberation, and decision-making out of it. Design an environment that helps you follow through:

- If you want to work out in the morning, lay out your clothes the night before.
- If you want to eat better, don't keep junk food in the house.
- If you want to write every day, schedule it, protect it, and make it non-negotiable.

If you want to stay consistent, build buffers, just like I did when I recorded twenty-two episodes before launching *The Learning Leader Show.* That way, no single disruption could derail the whole commitment. When I take my kids to their activities, we leave early. Not because we expect everything to go wrong but because it might. Maybe we hit traffic. Or someone needs to use the bathroom. That's OK. We're still on time. I'm productively paranoid about being late. Being on time shows respect to others. So, I go early.

The goal is always the same: eliminate failure as an option. Take *no* off the table.

Excuses are normal. If you want to live an uncommon life, you can't risk thinking like everyone else. Make a promise. Then, engineer a world where that promise is inevitable.

LUCK FAVORS THE PREPARED

In March 2016, Maggie Rogers was in her second semester of her senior year at NYU's Clive Davis Institute of Recorded Music. One day, the class had a special guest: Pharrell Williams. The thirteen-time Grammy winner was the school's artist-in-residence that semester and had stopped by to listen to student work and offer feedback.

The video of what happened broke the internet. When it was Maggie's turn to share, she presses play on a demo for a song called "Alaska." As the track unfolds, Pharrell's calm, even jaded expression shifts to surprise and delight. When it ends, he looks at her with astonishment: "I have zero notes for that." After comparing Rogers to music legends like the Wu Tang Clan and Stevie Wonder, he adds, *"I've never heard anyone like you before. I've never heard anything that sounds like that."*

Thanks to the viral video and Pharrell's support, Maggie Rogers went from being an unknown music student to an artist with major labels clamoring to sign her. To the outside world, this sudden change in career trajectory looked like luck. A viral moment that changed everything. But Rogers knew the truth because she'd been preparing for that moment for years.

"Part of success is having a good story," she told the *New York Times*. "[But] it meant that my many, many years of focus and hard work got kind of prepackaged into a Cinderella story." Maggie's overnight success resulted from diligence, discipline, and consistency. She'd been writing songs since she was thirteen. By seventeen, she had self-released an album. Rogers spent years honing her craft playing in bands, studying production, and immersing herself in music. She'd put in thousands of hours before a Grammy-winning producer happened to walk into her classroom.

Consistent preparation *creates* luck:

- A startup founder doesn't land a huge investor by chance. They spend years refining their pitch, studying their market, and showing up to every meeting prepared to deliver.
- A star athlete doesn't just happen to be in the right place at the right time. They put in years of training so that they're ready when the scout or the coach finally takes notice.
- A writer doesn't get a book deal out of nowhere. They've written draft after draft, shelved entire *manuscripts* as they honed their craft, just to become capable of creating something worth publishing.

It isn't a question of whether you'll ever get a lucky break. What matters is, will you be ready to catch it when it does?

THE THIRTY-YEAR OVERNIGHT SUCCESS

Most people get the Morgan Freeman story backward. They see the Oscar winner, the commanding voice, the epic movies like *The Shawshank Redemption*. What they miss is the brutal math of his life: thirty years of deliberate practice before his breakout role.

Three big things emerge from studying Morgan Freeman's path that challenge conventional wisdom about success:

First, his trajectory shows that career capital compounds. Each small role, from local theater productions to PBS children's shows was an investment in craft. He spent five years on *The Electric Company*, a children's show most actors would see as a career dead end. But it was daily repetition, a laboratory for developing his voice and presence.

The advantage of starting small is that you have the freedom to fail privately. While his peers chased big breaks, Freeman accumulated thousands of hours of practice in venues where mistakes had low costs. This is the opposite of what most people do, they want to start at the top (or want immediate promotions after a little bit of work), which oddly reduces their chances of getting there.

Second, Freeman's story reveals how success masks struggle. We see him now and think obviously he would succeed. But imagine being Morgan Freeman at forty-five. You've been acting for decades. Your peers have houses and retirement accounts. You're still taking small theater gigs. The ability to persist when the timeline is uncertain is rare because it's emotionally taxing. Most people can handle the work. Few can handle the wait.

Third, his path demonstrates that artificial timelines are the enemy of mastery. Society tells us success should come in our twenties, thirties, and forties. Morgan Freeman got his first Oscar nomination at fifty. His biggest roles came even later. The real barrier to achievement isn't age, it's quitting too early.

But here's what makes Freeman's story so interesting: he's not just an actor who got lucky after thirty years. He's an actor who got *better* for thirty years. While everyone else was trying to skip to the end, Freeman was doing the equivalent of thirty years of homework. Most people want the rewards of mastery without the costs of apprenticeship. As James Clear told me when we recorded a live show at Ohio University, *"Figure out the costs of success, and don't bargain over the price."* Being willing to look like a failure longer than your peers is one of the most valuable advantages you can have.

Too many people sit back and wait for others to recognize their potential. Hoping that an opportunity will just fall into their lap. That's not how it works. The people who win in any field don't wait for permission. They anticipate, act, and work out the bugs as they go. They make themselves easy to work with. They are reliable, responsive, and proactive. They pay attention to what others want (customers, clients, audiences, whoever) and deliver before being asked. That's how you become the person everyone wants to work with, hire, invest in, and support.

NEVER PHONE IT IN

The people who rise to the top are the ones who treat every opportunity as if it might be the one that ends up defining them. It comes down to a sense of urgency. You never know what a great performance might lead to, even if it seems like nobody's watching.

The late, legendary actor Philip Seymour Hoffman gave the following advice to aspiring performers: "If you get a chance to act in a room that somebody else has paid rent for, then you're given a free chance to practice your craft." His philosophy was simple but powerful: Every opportunity to perform is an opportunity to improve. Even if you're auditioning for a role that you know you won't get. Even if you're in a production that no one is watching. Even if the moment feels small. Treat it like it matters, because it does.

Some people only give their best when the stakes are high, but professionals give their best in every room, every time. That's how they raise the bar, not just for themselves but for everyone around them. For example, in the summer of 2023, the Dave Matthews Band played a concert in Noblesville, Indiana. A lightning storm was approaching fast. They knew that at any moment, the skies could open and end the show. So, they played every song as if it were their closer. No filler, no slow "go to the bathroom songs," just hit after hit, played with full intensity until the band was finally forced to unplug and leave the stage. I'd seen them live many times, but this was one of the best performances I'd witnessed. Why? Because they played with urgency, knowing each song could be their last.

Why wait for a storm to raise your level of intensity? What if you treated every presentation, every project, every opportunity like it might be your last shot at making an impression? You never know which effort will be the one that changes everything. A common mistake people make in pursuit of excellence is mistaking consistency for quality. Yes, showing up regularly is critical, but you can't just ship average work in the name of staying on schedule. That's why we trash 30 percent of the podcast recordings we do. If it doesn't meet the ever-increasing standards, it doesn't go out. Period. Publishing mediocre work in the name of consistency is a great way to lose.

The people and companies that endure, whether in

business, music, sports, or any other field, are the ones that refuse to let their standards slip. They are ruthless about quality. They don't just put something out because it's time. They put it out because it's excellent.

How do you ensure you're not phoning it in?

- **Use an outside evaluator.** A coach, mentor, or trusted peer can help you see when you're slipping into mediocrity. The best performers in the world have coaches.
- **Surround yourself with excellence.** When you work with people who have a high-quality bar, you naturally push yourself harder to keep up. Seek out those who challenge you.
- **Commit to exceeding your own standards.** Don't settle for being "good enough." Push to be exceptional. Even (*especially*) when nobody's watching.

Excellence is a habit like any other. You never know which swing will be the one that scores. That's why you never phone it in. The people who treat every opportunity like it's their last chance or big break, the ones who set the highest standards for themselves and refuse to lower them, are the ones who leave a mark.

The world loves an overnight success story. We celebrate the breakout athlete, the viral sensation, the entrepreneur who came out of nowhere with a billion-dollar idea. But these stories are crafted after the fact. What you never see in the highlight reel are the years of invisible effort that made that "sudden" breakthrough possible, the relentless, unsexy work that happened long before anyone was paying attention. Paul Rabil's rise to the top of lacrosse happened because he committed to taking one hundred shots a day, every day, for years. Important, lasting victories follow this pattern.

Overnight success is just long-term consistency in disguise.

Yes, we live in a culture that glorifies quick wins. Get-rich-quick schemes, instant fame, overnight transformations. People chase shortcuts, believing they can bypass the work. But reality doesn't operate that way. Imagine two people investing for retirement. One follows the slow, steady approach, putting money into index funds every month, letting time and compound interest do the heavy lifting. The other tries to hit it big, betting everything on high-risk plays in the hopes of an immediate windfall. How do their stories end? The inevitable outcome: the steady investor acquires security and real wealth, while the gambler loses everything. Are there exceptions? Of course. We are not counting on being the exception. We know the rule. The difference is it's hard. And most people don't want to do it. That's why we do.

Excellence works the same way. The people who build something great aren't the ones swinging wildly for home runs every time. They're the people who show up, do the work, and trust that effort will pay off eventually. Paul Rabil didn't need to make every shot. He just needed to take them. So, what are your one hundred shots a day? And more importantly, are you willing to show up and take those shots, even when nobody's watching? Because the real advantage isn't talent. It's *working a process*. The ones who commit to relentless consistency, no matter how small the action, are the ones who win.

Most of our failures happen because we treat important things like they're not that important. Think about the last time you had a goal that really mattered to you. Maybe it was starting a business, getting in shape, or learning a new skill. Now think about how you talked about it. Did you say "I'm going to do this" or "I'm thinking about maybe trying this"? The difference in language reveals a lot about your odds of making it happen.

We're casual in ways we don't even notice. We're casual with our mornings, letting them drift by instead of seizing them. We're casual with our attention, splitting it across a dozen things instead of focusing it like a laser on one. We're casual with our standards, accepting "good enough" when we know we could do better. The problem with casualness is that it compounds. Each small compromise feels insignificant on its own. Missing one workout doesn't matter. Skipping one day of practice won't hurt. Putting off that important conversation for another week is fine. But these decisions add up in ways that surprise us.

What's really happening here is that we're being unserious about the big goal. We'd rather dabble than commit. We'd rather keep our options open than go all in on one thing. And I get it. Being casual feels safer. It's psychologically easier to be casual about something important because you have a built-in excuse when you don't achieve it. "Well, I wasn't fully committed anyway." It's a hedge against disappointment. But this safety comes at a massive cost. The people who change the world don't dabble. They don't keep their options open. They pick something and get after it with relentless focus. They commit to the thing, even knowing they might give everything they have and still fall short. That's the fear casual people are avoiding: the possibility of full effort leading to failure anyway. Success and failure both happen gradually, then suddenly. You don't wake up one day and discover you're out of shape. You don't suddenly realize your business idea is dead. You don't instantly find yourself without the skills you need. These things happen slowly, through a thousand tiny choices that seemed harmless at the time.

The opposite is also true. Excellence emerges from the accumulation of small, consistent actions performed with obsessive attention to detail. Every person who has achieved something remarkable can trace it back to a period when they stopped being casual about what mattered most. This means identifying the few things that really matter and treating them with the seriousness they deserve. It means organizing your life around your priorities instead of hoping you can fit them into whatever time is left over.

The window of opportunity doesn't stay open forever. The market doesn't wait for you to get serious. Your health doesn't pause while you decide to start taking care of yourself. Time moves forward whether you're ready or not. If something matters enough to want, it matters enough to pursue with everything you have. Otherwise, you're just playing pretend with your own ambition. Casual effort gets casual results, not just in what you achieve, but in how you feel about yourself when you look back on what you did with your time. Your choice? Either treat your goals like they're worthy of obsession, or accept that they'll probably remain wishes.

YOUR ACTIONS ARE YOUR ARGUMENT

I've noticed that the most persuasive people rarely try to persuade anyone. They just live in a way that makes you think, "I want to be like that." The parent who consistently shows up early and stays late. The friend who is always quietly giving to others. The colleague who simply does what they say they'll do. The companies that succeed long-term are the ones that consistently deliver value to customers, even when nobody's watching. Think of your favorite teachers. For me, I had two professors at Ohio University that I loved, Dr. Daniel Modaff and Dr. J.W. Smith. They didn't inspire me giving motivational speeches. Instead, they quietly demonstrated what curiosity and learning looked like in practice. They genuinely cared for me as one of their students. Asked me questions about my life, showed an interest in me as a student athlete, and offered up to meet with me outside of class during their office hours every week. Their actions spoke far louder than any words.

There's a behavioral explanation for why examples work better than opinions. When someone tells you what to do, your brain immediately looks for reasons to disagree. It's a defense mechanism. But when someone shows you what's possible through their actions, your brain asks a different question: "How did they do that?" The same dynamic plays out in families, companies, and communities. The behavior that spreads is the one that works in practice, day after day, even when it's hard. People can sense when your actions match your words, and they pay attention to that alignment. It's a signal that cuts through the noise. In a world full of opinions, consistent behavior becomes rare and super valuable.

Focusing on your example rather than your opinion actually makes your opinion more powerful. When people see you living according to certain principles, they become curious about those principles. Your life becomes the marketing campaign for your ideas. But here's what most people miss: examples compound slowly, then suddenly. You might spend years modeling certain behaviors with no apparent impact. Then one day, someone mentions that watching you changed how they think about something. Your example reached critical mass.

The world changes through this quiet accumulation of individual choices. Not through the loudest voices or the most clever arguments, but from the steady demonstration of what's possible when someone actually lives their values. The world changes one person at a time, one choice at a time, one example at a time. Your life is your argument. Make it a good one.

BE A PRO

Early in my career, an older mentor told me, "Be a pro." I nodded like I understood, but I didn't know what he meant. As time has gone on, I've learned more about what it means to be a pro.

Being a pro is about recognizing that everything you do sends a signal about who you are. Show up early. Proofread your emails. Make your slides clean. Respond quickly. Be helpful without being asked. Be proactive. These seem trivial until you realize most people don't do them consistently. And consistency is where trust is built. The person who always shows up prepared becomes the person others want on their team. Small standards compound into big reputations. When you're sloppy, other people pay the price. Send an email with typos, and the reader has to decode what you meant. Show up late, and everyone else's time becomes less valuable. Run a disorganized meeting, and you've wasted collective human attention. Every time you make someone else's life worse, you're making a withdrawal from your reputation account. Every time you make their life better, you're making a deposit. People gravitate toward those who improve their lives, not those who create extra work.

Good lighting and audio for your Zoom calls aren't vanity. They're the basic tools of modern work. When you can't share your screen or your audio cuts out constantly, you're signaling that you haven't learned the fundamentals. It's like showing up to a construction site without knowing how to use your tools. The people who master these basics are showing respect for everyone else. The biggest myth about professionalism is that you have to choose between being fast and being good. The best professionals are both. They respond quickly because they've built systems to do it. They deliver quality because they've practiced enough to make quality their default. This is about being intentional.

The benefits of being a pro compound over time. The person known for running great meetings gets invited to more important meetings. The person who delivers clean work gets more interesting projects. The person who makes collaboration easy becomes indispensable. Better opportunities lead to better skills. Better skills lead to better opportunities. The gap between professionals and everyone else widens over time.

Being a pro is a choice about how you want to move through the world. You can see standards as constraints that limit your authenticity. Or you can see them as tools that amplify your impact. You can think details don't matter. You can also recognize that details often separate good from great. You can believe being casual makes you more relatable. Or you can understand that being reliable makes you more valuable. The older mentor who told me to "be a pro" understood something fundamental: being a pro is about creating the conditions for everyone to do their best work. In a world full of people who are just good enough, being great consistently is a superpower.

REFLECTION QUESTIONS

- When you think about your biggest goals, are you focusing on the outcome or the daily behaviors that would make that outcome inevitable?
- Looking at your current excuses for inconsistency, what systems could you build to make those excuses impossible?
- Are you waiting for someone to give you permission or an opportunity, or are you actively creating opportunities through your daily actions?
- How "casual" are you being with the things that matter most to you? What would change if you treated them with the obsession they deserve?
- When you look at your recent work or efforts, would you honestly say you're "phoning it in" or bringing professional-level intensity to everything you do?
- What story are you telling yourself about needing the "perfect moment" that's preventing you from starting the daily work today?

Take Action

- **Identify your one hundred shots and commit.** Pick one daily action that directly advances your most important goal. Make it specific, measurable, and completely within your control. Then do it every single day for the next thirty days, no exceptions.

- **Build your preparation systems.** Set up your environment to eliminate excuses before they happen. Lay out workout clothes, schedule your most important work for when you're freshest, remove distractions that derail consistency.

- **Stop waiting for permission.** Find one opportunity you've been hoping someone will give you and figure out how to create it yourself. Whether it's starting that project, reaching out to that person, or building that skill: act first, ask for forgiveness later.

- **Audit your casualness.** Write down your three most important goals, then honestly evaluate how seriously you're pursuing them. Are your actions matching the importance you claim these goals have?

- **Eliminate "phone it in" moments.** Pick one area where you've been giving less than your best effort and commit to bringing professional standards to it. Treat every interaction like it might be the one that changes everything.

- **Create accountability systems.** Find someone with their own daily commitment and text each other when you've completed your work. The goal isn't perfection; it's momentum and proof that you can keep promises to yourself.

- **Practice being a pro in small things.** Show up early to meetings, proofread every email, respond quickly to requests. Small standards compound into big reputations, and people notice who makes their lives better.

- **Document your compound progress.** Keep a simple log of your daily actions. Watch how small, consistent efforts add up over weeks and months. Use this evidence to fuel your belief that the long game works.

- **Design for the worst day.** Plan what you'll do when motivation is low, when circumstances are difficult, when you don't feel like showing up. Having a plan for your worst moments is what separates consistency from good intentions.

- **Raise your standards ruthlessly.** Stop accepting "good enough" from yourself. If your work doesn't meet your increasing standards, don't ship it just to maintain a schedule. Quality compounds faster than quantity.

6

Writing and Selling

The "Art" in Articulation

The highest-paid people in business do the same job, regardless of what their title is. They're professional translators. Not converting French to English. These people translate complexity into clarity. Your top salesperson translates product specs into customer benefits. The consultant who gets promoted translates technical analysis into executive summaries. The startup founder who raises millions translates their vision into investor language. The championship coach translates game strategy into player motivation and team chemistry. And here's the key: there are only two ways to become a professional translator. You can learn to write, or you can learn to sell. The most powerful people master both.

This book began as a selfish act. I hope it helps you. I hope it helps a lot of people. But the primary reason I started writing was to help myself. I write because I need to figure out what I actually think. Until I put words on paper, my ideas are just fuzzy thoughts bouncing around my head. The book-writing process forces clarity. You write a proposal. You work on it with your literary agent. You pitch publishers. You convince them to bet money on your idea. Every step requires you to get more specific about what you believe and why. There's no hiding behind vague concepts when your name goes on the cover.

Most people avoid writing because it's hard. Staring at a blank page feels terrible. Building an argument sentence by sentence is slow and frustrating (most of the time). AI changes this equation in interesting ways. It can generate ideas quickly. It can polish sentences. It can even build arguments that sound convincing. But AI can't figure out what you believe. That requires the kind of slow, uncomfortable thinking that happens when you sit alone with a problem for hours. AI is like having a great research assistant who never gets tired. Helpful, sure. But the assistant doesn't teach you *how to think*. That's still your job. And that's exactly why it's so valuable. Easy things don't change you.

THE DISCIPLINE OF NOTICING

One of my favorite writers, Henrik Karlsson, said:

> Good writing isn't about studying how great essays or poems look and then figuring out how to reverse engineer that (though that's part of it). Rather, it's about learning how to pay close attention to your thoughts and feelings and the concrete material-

ity of the world and mastering the craft so you can translate what you see onto the page.

The most impactful writers are great at noticing the world and putting words to their thoughts. They notice how people check their phones differently when they're anxious versus bored. They notice how people laugh differently when they're genuinely amused versus when they're trying to be polite. They notice the way someone's posture changes when they walk into a room where they know everyone versus one where they know no one.

This noticing is active work. It requires slowing down in a world that rewards speed. It means sitting with uncomfortable feelings instead of scrolling past them. It means asking, "Why does this matter?" when everyone else has moved on.

This is one of the reasons why I love studying great stand-up comedians. The best comedians are professional noticers. What makes a comedian great is their ability to see things that are hiding in plain sight. They take the mundane experiences we all share (like the weird social dance that happens when you're walking toward someone on a sidewalk) and hold them up to the light until we see them clearly for the first time. One that I've learned directly from is Nikki Glaser. For her, comedy isn't just about telling jokes. It's a daily commitment to observation: *"You need to pay attention constantly to everything to see what could potentially be a joke,"* she told me. "Sometimes, in the middle of a conversation with a friend, I'll tell them to hold on because I need to take out my phone and type something funny that I just saw. If you don't write it down, you won't remember it."

That's the mindset of a professional. The best comedians don't wait for inspiration. They hunt for it. They become professional "noticers of things." They don't assume a great joke will magically land in their lap. Instead, they work hard to prepare themselves to recognize one when it appears.

But noticing alone isn't enough. You can be the most observant person in the world, but if you can't translate those observations into words that land with readers, you're just having a private experience.

This is where craft comes in. Craft is the bridge between what you see and what others can understand. It's learning that some sentences need to be short. Others need to breathe. The magic happens when attention meets craft. When someone who has learned to see clearly also learns to write clearly. When private insights become shared understanding.

Think about the last piece of writing that stopped you in your tracks. It was because the author had noticed something true about the world or about being human, and they found a way to help you see it too. This is writing's real power. Not persuasion or entertainment, though it can do both. Its power is in making the invisible visible. In giving language to experiences that felt too complex or too personal to share.

Writing teaches us to see better. Seeing better (noticing things) makes for a better life. In a world full of noise and distraction, writing offers something rare: the discipline of deep attention and the reward of genuine connection and understanding. The writer in the coffee shop who watched steam rise from her cup understood something important. The world is already full of interesting things. The trick isn't learning to manufacture interest. It's learning to pay attention to what's already there.

THE HIDDEN CONNECTION

There's a reason Jeff Bezos and Ryan Petersen (and probably many others who have followed their lead) have their teams write six-page essays instead of giving PowerPoint presentations for their monthly reviews. You can pretend your way through slides. You can't fake your way through a coherent written argument about what's actually happening in your business.

I've felt what regular writing does to my brain. It makes me a better decision maker, a clearer thinker. It creates better outcomes in my life. The act of getting thoughts out of your head and onto the page rewires how you think. If you don't write regularly, you're missing one of the most powerful tools for improving your judgment. Most people won't do it because it's difficult. That's exactly why you should. Not only is it important to write, but there are incredible benefits to deep reading. Neuroscientists like Maryanne Wolf have discovered that reading literally rewires your brain, creating specialized areas, thickening your corpus callosum (the highway between brain hemispheres), and strengthening your ability to imagine alternative paths, remember details, and think through complex problems. Every time you engage in what Wolf calls "deep reading," the kind where you slow down, make connections, and let ideas percolate, you're developing the "contemplative dimension" of your brain that provides humans with the capacity to form insight and empathy.

I spent many years as a sales professional before becoming an author. The two jobs are fundamentally the same. That might sound odd at first. Both sales and writing require persistence through a lot of rejection. Both are also about persuasion, communication, and storytelling. To do well, both require an understanding of your audience and building trust.

A lot of people think sales is about pushy phone calls and writing is about sitting alone with fancy ideas. But strip away the stereotypes and you find the same core challenge: getting someone else to care about what you care about. Both sales and writing are rejection businesses. A good salesperson might close 10 percent of their prospects. A good writer might publish 10 percent of their pitches. The other 90 percent is just practice for getting better at the 10 percent that matters. Both require you to become a student of human nature. You have to understand what motivates people, what their problems are, what they really want versus what they say they want. You have to build trust with strangers who initially don't trust you.

Whether we realize it or not, everyone is in sales. Every email you send is a sales pitch. Every meeting is an attempt to sell an idea or persuade someone to go along with your plan. Every conversation with your spouse is you trying to sell them on your version of reality. The best salespeople I know are curious about people. They understand stories, human psychology, the power of the right word at the right time. While everyone has had a bad experience with a salesperson lying or trying to manipulate them, the real professional sellers know that great selling is about translation and helping others.

I had one of those moments recently that makes you realize how seemingly random events connect to deeper truths about how we think and grow. During the summer of 2024, I spoke with Ryan Holiday about recording our ninth podcast episode together. When he suggested doing it in person at his studio in Bastrop, Texas, I booked my flight that day.

As we talked for seventy-five minutes, I kept hearing a slight creak from the desk we were sitting at. *"This is Joan Didion's old desk,"* Ryan told me when I asked about it. *"This is where she wrote a lot of her best work."*

It's funny how these moments work. Up until then, Didion was just a name to me. But sitting there, feeling the subtle movements of the desk where she formed some of her most important thoughts, I started thinking about how we process ideas. Didion had figured out something fundamental about thinking that applies to everything from decision-making to understanding ourselves. "I write entirely to find out what I'm thinking," she said. Writing doesn't just record thoughts, it creates them.

Think about that for a moment. Most of us assume we know what's in our heads until we try to explain it to someone else. Didion took this further: "Had I been blessed with even limited access to my own mind there would have been no reason to write." She understood that even our own thoughts are somewhat inaccessible until we do the work of putting them on paper.

The gap between what you think you know and what you actually know is only revealed when you try to explain it to someone else. Writing is that explanation in its purest form.

A lot of us walk around with a false sense of understanding. We nod along to ideas and concepts, thinking we grasp them fully. But there's a big difference between feeling like you understand something and actually understanding it well enough to explain it clearly. Writing exposes that gap immediately. The ideas I'm most certain about often crumble when I try to write them down. What seemed like a coherent argument in my head turns into a collection of half-formed thoughts when forced onto the page. This is a good thing. It's discovery.

The magic happens in that moment of realization: "Oh, I don't actually understand this as well as I thought." That's when real learning begins. Writing regularly creates a feedback loop for your thinking. You write something down, realize it's not quite right, refine it, try again. Over time, this process trains your brain to think more clearly even before you start writing.

If you don't know where to start, the best way to learn is to write about what fascinates you. Your curiosity is the ultimate guide. When you write about topics that genuinely interest you, two things happen: you learn more deeply, and your excitement becomes contagious.

Writing driven by curiosity creates a feedback loop. Questions lead to partial answers. Those answers spark new questions. Before long, you've developed unique insights simply by following your interests. The people who develop the deepest expertise don't necessarily start with grand ambitions. They just keep writing about what interests them, letting their curiosity compound over time.

Clear thinking requires writing. And the best writing happens when you're chasing what you most want to understand.

THE ART OF SELLING THROUGH STORY

Writing changes you from the inside out. It sharpens your thinking, clarifies your beliefs, and forces you to confront the gaps in your understanding. But there's something else that happens when you develop this skill. You become better at moving others.

Think about what writing actually requires. You start with a jumbled mess of thoughts and somehow organize them into something another person can follow. You anticipate their questions before they ask them. You help turn their existing knowledge into new ideas. This is what great selling requires.

The funny thing about persuasion is that it rarely happens through pure information. Some people like to say, "Facts don't care about your feelings." And while that may be true, it's shortsighted thinking. Humans are not always rational. The facts alone aren't usually convincing enough to change someone's mind. But stories do. We think we make decisions based on facts, but we actually make them based on feelings, then use facts to justify what we already believe. This isn't a bug in human reasoning. It's the operating system.

The person who tells the most compelling story usually ends up running things. It doesn't matter if you have the best data or the smartest strategy if you can't explain why it matters in a way that sticks. Stories move people in ways that spreadsheets never will, and the leader is almost always whoever can paint the cleanest picture of what tomorrow should look like.

I learned this while working as a VP of sales at a big company. My teammates who built the strongest client relationships were the ones who could explain complex ideas through simple stories. Warren Buffett understands this well. His annual letters are master classes in storytelling. He could bombard shareholders with financial metrics and industry jargon. Instead, he uses folksy analogies about baseball and hamburgers. The result? He's created an army of long-term shareholders who stick with him through market cycles when most investors panic.

Stories are how humans actually process information, even when we pretend we're being rational and data driven. You start with a hunch about how the world works, then go find the numbers that make your case. The most compelling narratives often have a structure that our brains are wired to follow. There's a status quo, then a conflict that disrupts it, followed by a resolution that creates a new understanding. This three-act structure exists across cultures because it mirrors how we experience life: things are fine, disruption happens, then we have a resolution and we're better than where we were. Stories are easier to remember, easier to relate to, and emotionally persuasive. They create memorable moments that stick with us. We remember great stories years later, but we forget the statistics from yesterday's news.

When trying to persuade, resist immediately leading with data. Instead, address their concerns and then share the specific story that changed your perspective. A journey from shared skepticism to new understanding is more compelling than declaring what someone should believe.

Facts inform. Stories transform. The most effective communicators understand this balance.

IF WE'RE ALL GONNA EAT, SOMEONE HAS TO SELL

Ken Griffin, founder/CEO of Citadel (a multinational hedge fund), once told a story about one of the most overlooked truths in business and life. His former physics teacher, who later became his business partner in Chicago, kept a small plaque behind his desk. It wasn't expensive or flashy. Just a sign that read: "If we're all gonna eat, someone has to sell."

We love to talk about ideas, innovation, talent. But none of it matters if you can't convince someone else that it's valuable. Because everything in business and life involves selling. You're selling to customers. To new hires. To investors. To teammates. Most of the time, you're not even selling a product. You're selling a vision. A feeling. A sense of trust. You're selling the belief that the future will be better than the past if we just keep going.

Everything is selling. When you interview for a job, you're selling yourself. When you pitch an idea to your boss, you're selling a change. When you ask someone on a date, you're selling a future together. If you think that you don't work in sales, you're lying to yourself. We are all in sales. Every single day. Ken Griffin understood this early. It's part of the reason he became worth north of forty billion dollars.

That means you're going to hear the word *no* a lot. My first job after college was as a new business telephonic sales rep at LexisNexis. I was responsible for calling small law firms and convincing attorneys that they should use our products for their online legal research instead of our competitors'. It was brutal: sixty cold calls a day, many more cold emails, and some days, I would hear *no* 100 percent of the time. I'd get hung up on, yelled at, ignored, or told straight up, *"Stop calling me."* It's hard not to take it personally. But you have to keep going. Each no is one step closer to a yes. If you weren't able to forge ahead in the face of all the rejection, you had to go somewhere else. But that job was the best introduction to life that I could have ever had. It conditioned me to deal with adversity and keep going. It's made every job since then seem much easier.

Rich Gotham, President of the Boston Celtics, told me the same thing. His first job was a sales rep at NCR corporation in Dayton, Ohio. He was trained well, but he still got rejected all the time. When we spoke, he said, "That made all the jobs I've had after that easier."

The best leaders aren't necessarily the smartest people in the room. They're the ones who can take an idea and make other people care about it. They can paint a picture of the future that feels both possible and necessary. They understand that having a great idea is only a fraction of the battle. The rest is convincing other people that your great idea is actually great.

SELLING A VISION

In 2001, Adam Levine asked guitar player, James Valentine, to abandon a working situation for an unproven opportunity. Adam's band, Kara's Flowers, had already experienced commercial failure with their previous album and now they were proposing to completely reinvent themselves. From Valentine's perspective, this was risky. But Levine understood something about human psychology: people don't buy products; they buy better versions of themselves.

In an April 2025 interview with Howard Stern, Levine shared his approach: "I can be persistent especially when I feel things. I can be very passionate. I can be intense." He knows that conviction is contagious. When someone believes something deeply enough, that belief becomes a form of social proof. His intensity was authenticity expressed with such force that it became compelling.

And then he said to Valentine, *"You're gonna regret not doing this for the rest of your life."* This is loss aversion at work. Instead of just selling the upside potential, he was highlighting the cost of missing out. The pain of regret is often more motivating than the promise of gain. Adam was also great at removing friction from the decision. As he told Stern: "I will come to your house and help you pack your bags. Move into my house."

He wasn't just asking Valentine to take a leap of faith; he was helping make that leap easier. The process worked because Levine understood that big decisions rarely happen in single moments. Valentine described it as "very much like I was cheating on my (other) band, we were having sort of an affair." This gradual courtship allowed trust to build over time. Levine was patient enough to let the relationship develop naturally while maintaining consistent pressure toward his goal. What's shrewd is how Levine leveraged social proof. According to his account on Stern's show, "the whole band wore him down." This was a coordinated campaign. When multiple people are aligned behind the same vision, it creates momentum that becomes hard to resist.

And most importantly, Levine was selling something he genuinely believed in. His confidence came from deep conviction about what they could accomplish together. Valentine later noted that his jazz background gave him "the right tools to complement the hip-hop, soul, and R&B sounds they were exploring." Levine had identified a genuine need and found the perfect person to fill it. The compound effect of Levine's sales skills in that moment created decades of excellence. But it worked because he combined genuine conviction with smart psychology, persistent effort with patience, and bold vision with support from others. A commonality I've found with excellent leaders over the course of the decade-plus of interviews I've done is they have 100 percent conviction in what they're doing, and they're exceptional at selling others to join them to help achieve the vision. That conviction is contagious and works as a great tool to inspire others to follow along. Maroon 5 has been together for twenty-five years. They've made seven albums, earned hundreds of millions of dollars, toured the world, and brought joy to countless people with music that just sticks with you. All because someone believed deeply in what they were building and knew how to get others to believe in it too.

THE PRICE AND THE PRIZE

Here's what I've learned from sitting at Joan Didion's desk, from getting hung up on thousands of cold calls, from hearing Adam Levine convince a guitarist to abandon everything for an uncertain future: the people who shape the world are the ones who can turn thoughts into words, and words into action.

Writing and selling are the same skill expressed in different contexts. Both demand that you understand your audience better than they understand themselves. Both force you to confront the gap between what you think you know and what you can actually prove. This is why most of the leaders I've interviewed have a writing practice. Writing is a forcing function for clear thinking. And clear thinking is what separates good leaders from great ones.

This is about recognizing that every important conversation in your life is an act of persuasion. Every email is a sales pitch. Every presentation is an attempt to move someone from where they are to where you want them to be. The price of becoming someone who can do this well is the discomfort of facing your own unclear thinking on paper. The reward is influence. Real influence. The kind that comes not from authority or manipulation, but from the power of real persuasion.

Your thoughts, refined through writing, become the tools you use to build the life you want. Your words, sharpened through getting the reps, help turn your vision into reality. Words are how we turn thoughts into action, ideas into reality, strangers into customers, and confusion into clarity.

This is about *becoming a professional translator.* Writing is how you figure out what you think. Selling is how you get others to think it too. The first creates clarity. The second creates change. You need both if you want to build anything that puts a positive dent in the world.

REFLECTION QUESTIONS

- What important decision are you avoiding because you haven't written down what you actually think about it? Remember, you don't know what you believe until you get the fuzzy thoughts out of your head onto the page.
- When you notice something interesting about human behavior, do you write it down? The best writers and sellers are professional noticers who see what others miss. They document their lives (at a minimum in a journal for themselves).
- How often do you discover that your "brilliant" ideas fall apart the moment you try to explain them on paper? Writing exposes the gap between what you think you know and what you actually understand.
- When you try to convince someone of something you deeply believe, why do they walk away unconvinced? Your internal certainty means nothing if you can't translate it into their language.
- What's the most complex thing you understand that you can't explain simply to someone outside your field? If you can't make it simple, you don't own the idea.
- Think about the last time someone changed your mind about something important. Did they overwhelm you with data or tell you a story that made you feel what they felt?
- Why do some people walk into a room and get everyone aligned around their vision while others get ignored? Conviction without translation (usually telling an interesting story) is just noise in someone else's head.

Take Action

- **Write to discover.** Every morning, spend twenty to thirty minutes writing about a problem you're trying to solve. Write to find out what you think.
- **Become a professional noticer.** Carry a notebook (or use your phone) for one week and write down three specific ob-

servations about human behavior each day. Include the weird social dances, the subtle contradictions, the things hiding in plain sight.

- **Practice explaining complexity simply.** Take the most technical part of your job and practice explaining it to people outside your field until they nod with genuine understanding (not polite confusion). This is your competitive advantage waiting to be developed.

- **Study rejection (like a scientist).** Track every *no* you get this month. Note what you asked for, how you asked, and what you think went wrong. Most people avoid rejection so completely they never learn what actually works.

- **Lead with their problem, not your solution.** Before your next important pitch, write down the issues the other person is dealing with. Think about it from their perspective, not just with what you want to tell them about your brilliant idea.

- **Master the art of contagious conviction.** Find something you believe deeply and practice explaining why it matters until people start interrupting you with questions instead of waiting politely for you to finish. Work on being more clear.

- **Remove friction from other people's decisions.** Next time you ask for something important, eliminate every barrier that makes saying yes harder. Make the right choice the easy choice, like Adam Levine offering to pack the bags.

- **Write until your thinking gets clearer.** Once a week, pick a topic you think you understand completely and write one thousand words about it. Keep going until you realize something you didn't expect. That's when real learning happens.

- **Practice selling vision, not features.** Instead of explaining what your idea does, practice explaining the specific future it creates and why that future matters more than people realize. People buy transformation, not products.

- **Become the translator.** Identify the most confusing part of your industry and commit to becoming the person who can explain it clearly to anyone. In a world full of complexity, simple explanations are a superpower.

PART III

LEAD

7

Trust Your Wings

Leading Without Permission

One of the most common questions I get from young professionals is about promotions. How do you get noticed? What gets you ahead? How do you position yourself for bigger roles? I've watched lots of careers develop over the years. Some people rocket up the ladder while others with similar talent stay stuck. There's a story in those differences.

First, be excellent in your current role. I don't care what it is. When I was a teenager, my first job was as an intern for a guy who owned a transportation company. One day I'd be painting the walls of a warehouse, the next I was getting him groceries. My mission was clear: paint those walls perfectly and make sure to get him exactly what he wanted from Kroger. Regardless of what your job is, be excellent at it. Nothing else matters if you haven't gotten this right. This won't guarantee a promotion, but failing at it promises you won't get one. You can't focus on the next thing without being great at the current one.

Next, we have an uncomfortable truth. Your employer pays you to do your job, not to prepare you for the next one. That preparation is your responsibility. Learn what skills are needed to be excellent at the role you want and develop them *on your own time*, not during company working hours. The market rewards skills it values, not complaints about lack of opportunity. You want to become a better writer? Read and write every morning before work. A better speaker in front of a group? Go to improv classes on the weekend. The skills that create career value don't always develop between the hours of eight and five. They're built in the margins of life. The people who get promoted choose to do extra work and develop additional skills in their own free time.

Third, become a *surplus-value* employee. Companies keep and promote people who create more value than they extract. This doesn't only apply to revenue-generating roles such as product development or sales; it's the same whether you work in marketing, human resources, inventory management, or building maintenance. Mentor others, solve problems before they become crises, and make the company culture better. When you consistently deliver multiple times what you cost, your promotion becomes a rational business decision.

The people who get promoted fastest are busy doing excellent work, learning constantly, and making everyone around them better. The system works because excellence creates opportunity, skills create options, and value creation increases demand for you. These are some of the compounding habits that help you reach your potential.

And when all three compound together, promotion stops being something you ask for and starts being something companies beg you to accept.

TRUST YOUR WINGS

After watching lots of people navigate career transitions, economic downturns, and industry disruption, I've noticed something that separates those who thrive from those who merely survive. It comes down to a fundamental misunderstanding about security. Most people think security comes from finding the right external circumstances and then protecting those circumstances from changing. The stable company, the growing industry, the appreciative boss. They spend a bunch of energy trying to make these things permanent. But here's what I've seen: The people who weather change best don't try to prevent it. They prepare for it. There's a reason a bird can sit calmly on a swaying branch during a storm. Not because it trusts the branch, but because it trusts its wings.

Here are two different approaches to career security:

External security: betting everything on conditions you can't control staying favorable.

Internal security: developing capabilities that create value regardless of circumstances.

The difference in outcomes is big. External security seekers spend their careers managing risk through avoidance. They choose "safe" industries, "stable" companies, predictable roles. When change comes, they struggle because their entire strategy was built on change not coming.

Internal security builders spend their careers managing risk through capability development. They assume change is inevitable and prepare by becoming adaptable. When change comes, they often find better opportunities because they're equipped to handle new situations. When the company my dad worked for got acquired, a lot of his colleagues were scared of the new bosses. Fearing layoffs, they started updating their résumés and looking for jobs. My dad did something different. He aggressively asked for meetings with the new leaders with the intention to help them make the acquisition smoother. He embraced the changes, went on offense, and ended up earning a much bigger role than he had prior to the acquisition. When others are scared and play defense, trust in the skills you've built, go for what you want, and focus on how you can add value to others' lives. That's what my dad did for the new bosses. He made their lives easier.

Internal security is not glamorous. It's daily skill development when others are relaxing. It's taking on challenging projects when easier ones are available. It's learning from failure when others are avoiding it. But the compound effect is real. Over time, you develop *professional antifragility.* Instead of being damaged by change, you're strengthened by it. New challenges become growth opportunities. Market shifts become competitive advantages.

The most secure people I know are the ones who could leave their current situation tomorrow and be fine. When you don't need your current job desperately, you become more valuable to that opportunity. Companies want to retain people who choose to stay, not people who stay because they have no other options. Personal relationships follow the same pattern. The best partnerships are between people who want to be together, not people who need to be together. Developing internal security isn't easy. It requires consistent effort over long periods. It means facing uncertainty instead of avoiding it. It means investing in yourself when that investment has no guaranteed return. Most people choose external security because it feels easier in the short term. Find the right nest and protect it. But this strategy becomes increasingly expensive over time because you're always fighting forces you can't control. Building wings is harder upfront but better over time because you're investing in capabilities that compound.

YOU ARE THE TRAFFIC

> I got bored with people saying, "the world is shit." It's kind of like when people say, "oh, the traffic is so bad." I'm like, *"You are the traffic."* You can't sit there and say, "Oh man, the traffic was horrible. I'm sorry I was late." You *are traffic. You're in it. Without you, there would be no traffic. So, if you're sitting here being like, "the world is shit," it's like, you are* the world. You have to take that responsibility. So, I focused on making sure that everything I'm making is shit I wish was in the world.

This quote from actor/musician, Donald Glover, has been living in my head for a while. There's something useful about the traffic analogy that cuts through our tendency to separate ourselves from the problems we complain about. We all do it. We talk about *the economy* as if it's some external force acting upon us, not the collective result of our decisions. We say *society* as if we're not active participants in creating it each day. But Glover's thoughts apply far beyond traffic jams and societal complaints. It speaks to a truth about excellence and ownership.

Glover's quote also reminds me of Jose Andrés, the chef who grew frustrated with traditional disaster relief efforts. Rather than just criticizing the system, he founded World Central Kitchen in 2010. When Hurricane Maria devastated Puerto Rico in 2017, traditional aid organizations struggled with logistics. Meanwhile, Andrés and his team served over three million meals.

"We need to be more ambitious," he told NPR in 2020. "Is it a problem that we have hungry people in America, in the world? Yes, it's a problem. But the problem has a solution."

That's ownership. And ownership is the difference between work that feels like a burden and work that feels like an expression of who you are. This principle shows up more once you start looking for it. Yvon Chouinard founded Patagonia after being dissatisfied with the climbing equipment available in the 1970s. He didn't just complain about the damaging pitons that scarred rock faces, he created reusable climbing hardware, then built an entire company around the ethos of environmental responsibility. "Earth is now our only shareholder," Chouinard wrote in an open letter when, in 2022, he took it to another level by transferring company ownership to a trust and nonprofit dedicated to fighting climate change and protecting nature.

Similarly, architect Bjarke Ingels got tired of the false choice between practical but boring buildings versus artistic but impractical ones. Instead of just criticizing both approaches, he pioneered what he calls "hedonistic sustainability," creating buildings that are both environmentally responsible and fun to live in. "Sustainability can't be like some sort of a moral sacrifice or political dilemma or a philanthropical cause. It has to be a design challenge," Ingels explained in his 2011 TED Talk.

Ownership starts with a shift in perspective from critic to creator, from passive observer to active participant. The most reliable path to doing excellent work isn't complaining about what's missing or what's broken. It's recognizing that you are an active participant in the world, not just a passive observer of it. When we internalize this message, we stop waiting for others to fix things and start asking ourselves what we can contribute. We move from "Someone should make a better X" to "I will make a better X." This mindset shift doesn't guarantee success or recognition. But it will help your work have purpose beyond external validation.

The next time you're complaining about something, remember, you're not stuck in traffic. *You are traffic.* That realization, uncomfortable as it may be, is the first step toward creating work that matters. The world doesn't get better when we point out its flaws. It improves when we take responsibility for addressing them through what we do. That's the essence of ownership.

This isn't about grand, sweeping gestures. Start small. The next time you find yourself thinking "Someone should fix this," replace that idea with "How can I make this better?" If your workplace has a broken process, don't just complain about the problem; propose a solution. If your community lacks something important, do something about it. Keep a notebook of things you wish existed, then pick one item and bring it to life. This shift from critic to creator doesn't happen overnight. It's a muscle developed through consistent practice, identifying gaps between what is and what could be, then personally stepping into those gaps. The results may not be perfect at first, but the act itself transforms both your work and your relationship to the world around you. Excellence isn't measured by outcomes alone, but by the courage to take ownership when it would be easier to simply complain.

Once you've accepted that you are part of creating the world around you, the natural question becomes: how do you act on that responsibility?

LEAD WITHOUT PERMISSION

In the summer of 1998, a Pixar animator typed a simple command: rm*. In an instant, Woody began to disappear from the server. Then Buzz. Then the entire digital universe of *Toy Story 2* was gone. This wasn't just an "Oops, my bad!" moment. It was the digital equivalent of watching $100 million and 20,000 hours of creative work vanish in seconds. The backup system, they quickly discovered, had been silently failing for months. The studio had been creating without a safety net, only nobody knew until it broke.

But here's where it gets interesting. Galyn Susman, a technical director, had recently had a baby. Because of her newborn, she'd been working from home and, crucially, keeping a copy of the film on her personal computer. When disaster struck, Susman didn't wait for orders. She didn't email her supervisor asking for permission to suggest a solution. She simply called in and said: "I have the files."

They wrapped her computer in blankets, literally treating a hard drive with the care of a newborn, and drove it back to Pixar headquarters like it contained the nuclear codes. That computer, which nobody had authorized Susman to use for backups, saved Pixar millions. *Toy Story 2* went on to gross about $500 million worldwide.

Ed Catmull, Pixar's co-founder, would later distill the moral of this near catastrophe into nine words: *"You never have to ask permission to take responsibility."*

I enjoy learning about how organizations work. We create elaborate chains of command, authorization protocols, and permission structures. Yet in a crisis, all that matters is who steps up. The most valuable people on a team are those who spot problems before they are problems and fix them before being asked.

The irony? Susman might have technically violated company policy by having those files at home. But when digital Woody was vanishing byte by byte, nobody cared about the rule book. This idea extends far beyond animation studios. Consider your own workplace: How many problems linger because people are waiting for someone else to fix them? How often do opportunities pass because they don't fit neatly into someone's job description? The most impactful organizations I've studied share a common trait: they're filled with leaders (regardless of titles) who act like owners rather than employees. These people spot and implement solutions without requiring a committee's approval. They speak up when processes don't make sense.

The odd thing about authority is that those who wait for it often never receive it, while those who take responsibility are eventually given the authority to match. The beauty of this is its simplicity. You don't need anyone's signature to become a valuable member of the team. You just need to be the one who says, "I'll handle it" before anyone asks you to. But Galyn Susman's story reveals something deeper about how careers actually work. The people who get ahead aren't necessarily the smartest or most talented. They're the ones who understand that organizations are just collections of humans trying to solve problems, and people are grateful to anyone who makes their problems go away.

This is why some careers take off while others plateau despite similar credentials. It has little to do with what school they attended or what score they got on a test. It comes down to whether they see problems as opportunities to prove their worth or obstacles that someone else should handle. The math is simple. In any organization, there are always more problems than people assigned to solve them. The person who voluntarily takes on the messy situations that don't fit neatly into anyone's job description, becomes indispensable through pure utility. When the building is on fire, nobody checks whether the person with the fire extinguisher has the proper authorization to use it.

THE COMMITMENT ADVANTAGE

Optionality is overrated. Everyone's obsessed with keeping their options open, but options without execution aren't very useful. The people winning are the ones who picked something and got really, really good at it. Commitment is a competitive advantage. (Remember from my conversation with Ed Latimore: "I didn't just dabble.")

Palmer Luckey, the founder of Oculus VR (sold to Facebook for two billion dollars) and now defense technology company Anduril, sees this mentality as a mistake. "At some point, in business and in life and in romance, you have to commit to a path," said the thirty-three-year-old Luckey. "A lot of my peers in the tech industry do not share this philosophy . . . They're always pursuing everything with optionality. 'Oh, I need to be able to raise money from anybody. I need to be able to sell my business in any way. I need to have liquidity in any way. I need to make sure that I'm not closing myself off to future romantic partners. I need to make sure I've got my options open. I need to make sure that I'm not going to buy a house and settle down in one place and lock myself down. Oh, having children. I don't know. Maybe I'm not ready to commit to that path.'"

But this strategy of never-ending hedging comes with a cost. When we keep one foot out the door, we never fully enter the room. When we're always looking over our shoulder for better options, we never fully focus on the opportunity in front of us. The energy we spend maintaining our escape routes is energy we're not investing in forward progress.

I learned this lesson firsthand. A few years after starting *The Learning Leader Show*, I was at a crossroads. The show's success had opened unexpected doors: keynote speaking opportunities, leadership development training requests, and executive coaching offers. But I was still working as the vice president of sales at a large company, leading a team responsible for over five hundred million dollars in annual revenue. I was trying to do it all, and I started to notice a bad pattern: *I was becoming average at everything instead of excellent at anything.*

The choice became clear: either scale back my growing media presence and the opportunities it created or leave corporate America to focus entirely on this accidental business I'd built. I chose the latter. What could happen if I gave everything I had to build a media and leadership consulting business? I wasn't sure, but I knew that 100 percent commitment was the only way to find out.

The first couple of years after making that choice in late

2017 were tough. While I had good clients, the money didn't match my VP salary and bonuses. But each year since making that commitment has been better than the one before it. Now, I can't imagine doing anything else. There was simply no way to discover this path's potential without first making that complete commitment and sacrifice.

Sometimes, the only way to know if something will work is to eliminate all other options and throw yourself fully into the pursuit. When we commit to a path, be it a relationship, a business, or a craft, we unlock levels of achievement that are impossible to reach with one foot out the door. But commitment is scary because it means saying no to other possibilities. It means accepting that we can't have everything, be everything, and do everything. It requires us to make peace with the paths not taken. It also opens us up to look stupid. I vividly remember a conversation with a mentor I trust, who told me I was crazy to leave a VP role at a great company, "Man, you've got a great gig. Why would you give that up? That's crazy. Is Miranda [my wife] really okay with this?" He might have been right, and I would have felt like an idiot if this hadn't worked out. That's part of the risk of committing to something. You might look stupid for doing it.

Maybe this is why our culture has developed such an attachment to optionality. It feels safer. Less painful. We tell ourselves we're being smart, strategic, keeping our powder dry. But often, we're just avoiding the discomfort of commitment, the vulnerability of going all-in on something that matters. The truth is that big achievements require complete commitment. It demands that we close off escape routes and fully own our choices. In a world obsessed with keeping options open, the courage to commit might be the rarest and most valuable asset of all.

But commitment to a path raises an important question. How do you build the relationships and opportunities that will help you succeed along that path? The answer might surprise you.

THE BEST NETWORKING TOOL? MAKE SOMETHING GREAT

Let me tell you about two musicians. One spends her days methodically messaging industry executives, sending carefully crafted emails to A&R representatives, and attending every networking event where someone important might appear. She has a perfect pitch deck of her music career and business cards with her SoundCloud link. The other spends those same hours in a room writing songs that matter to her. Some days the songs are terrible. Other days they're just OK. Occasionally, they're really good.

The first musician's networking strategy might work. The second musician isn't even trying to network.

Here's what happened to Gracie Abrams: In 2023, she joined Taylor Swift's record-breaking Eras Tour as an opening act, performing in massive stadiums for crowds of 70,000+ fans night after night. It was a career-defining opportunity, the kind that launches careers into new orbits. How did she land this coveted spot? She didn't chase it. Years earlier, Gracie was writing songs in her bedroom, recording voice memos, and eventually releasing music that felt honest to her. Fortunately, Taylor Swift heard some of that early work and became a fan. She started promoting Gracie's music, and eventually the two formed a genuine creative connection. They collaborated on a song for Abrams' debut album, with Swift as a co-writer. When the time came to select opening acts for the biggest tour in music history, Taylor chose someone whose work had already spoken for itself.

This looks like a perfect story about how great work beats traditional networking. And there's truth to that. But like most business stories, it's messier than it appears.

At first glance, you might think that I'm trying to convince you that networking is bad or that you can ignore it completely. But that's not my point. The lesson is that most impactful leaders, creators, and innovators do two things at once: they create great work, and they're thoughtful about building relationships and getting noticed. The good stuff happens when these overlap. Gracie Abrams didn't just write songs in isolation. She recorded them. Released them. She put them where people could find them. She built something worth discovering and then made sure it could be discovered. The problem with traditional networking isn't that it never works. It's that it often puts the cart before the horse. You're trying to build relationships *before* you've built something worth talking about. But here's where the "just focus on your work" advice gets tricky: it assumed you have a way for the right people to find that work. If you're writing songs in your bedroom but never sharing them, Taylor Swift will never hear them. If you're building software that solves real problems but keeping it to yourself, the people who need it never know it exists.

The most effective approach combines both strategies in a sequence that feels natural. First, you build something genuinely useful or beautiful. Then you share it thoughtfully with people who might care. You're not networking for the sake of networking. You're connecting around something real. This requires patience and resources that many people don't have, the ability to work without immediate returns, access to tools for creation and distribution, and often some financial cushioning to sustain the long game. These aren't small advantages. The uncomfortable truth is that pure "just make great work" advice works best when you already have some platform or credibility. If you're starting from zero, waiting passively for discovery can leave you waiting forever. Instead, try this: create something valuable, share it where the right people might see it, and be genuinely helpful when opportunities to connect arise. Don't ignore relationship-building, but make sure you have something worth building relationships around. Doing great work doesn't eliminate the need for human connections. It helps make those connections feel natural and sustainable. People want to help others whose work they respect. They don't want to support people whose only skill is asking for help. The most effective networking doesn't feel like networking at all. It feels like sharing something you're proud of with people who might appreciate it.

The power of this approach comes from three aspects that conventional networking can never replicate:

1. **It filters for the right people.** When you create exceptional work (publishing your writing online, winning a big case, helping others consistently wherever you work), you naturally attract people who genuinely value what you do. Would you rather have one genuine connection with someone who deeply appreciates your work, or twenty superficial connections with people who took your business card to be polite?
2. **It establishes relationship leverage.** In traditional networking, you're often the one asking for something: attention, opportunity, mentorship. But when someone

discovers your work and reaches out because it impressed them, the dynamic is reversed. They're coming to you because they see value in what you create. This shift in relationship leverage changes everything.

3. **It scales in ways traditional networking cannot.** There are physical limits to how many networking events you can attend or cold emails you can send. But great work can reach anyone, anywhere, at any time, even while you sleep.

Gracie Abrams' music could be discovered by Taylor Swift whether Abrams was performing, sleeping, or writing her next song. The work itself became her networking agent, working 24/7 with perfect authenticity. This approach to connection through creation isn't limited to music. It works in every field. (By the way, I know the cynics are saying, "It sure helps that Gracie has a famous dad [JJ Abrams]. I 100 percent agree with you. With that said, Taylor Swift doesn't care about the musician's parents when they're onstage as her opening act. She wants someone who will put on a great show.)

The greatest networking happens when you stop trying to network and instead focus on creating work worthy of the people you want to connect with.

Of course, this isn't easy. It requires:

Patience: You might work in obscurity for years before the right people notice.

Vulnerability: You have to share work that might be rejected or ignored.

Trust: You must believe that exceptional work eventually finds its audience.

Persistence: You need to keep creating even when there's no immediate payoff.

But this path, though longer and less certain, leads to connections that are more meaningful, more valuable, and more lasting than any you could make through traditional networking alone. The best introduction letter you'll ever have is doing excellent work and creating something of value to others. Once you've committed to a path and begun creating work that matters, you'll inevitably need to navigate the complex web of relationships and internal challenges that come with any meaningful pursuit. That's where execution skills become crucial.

"GOOD NEWS OFTEN, BAD NEWS EARLY, NEVER ANY SURPRISES"

During one of the meetings with my Learning Leader Circle a few years ago, we were focused on how we all can better manage up. Fellow member, Stephanie (Steph) Wernick Barker, said, *"Good news often. Bad news early. And never any surprises."*

People hate uncertainty more than they hate bad news. Your boss can handle problems. What they can't handle is being blindsided by something they should have known about weeks ago. The ability to manage relationships with those above you isn't some corporate game. It's a core skill that separates people who advance from those who stagnate, regardless of their technical abilities. When done well, it reduces friction, builds trust, and creates conditions where everyone can do their best work.

This is a useful framework for communication that deserves a deeper look:

Good news often: Sharing wins, progress, and positive developments regularly keeps your boss informed and builds confidence in your abilities. Don't wait for formal reviews to highlight accomplishments. A quick email about meeting a milestone or receiving positive client feedback takes minimal effort but keeps your contributions visible. I liked sending these notes to my boss every Friday morning (or a few hours before our scheduled one-on-ones).

Bad news early: *Problems don't get better with age.* When issues arise, addressing them immediately gives your boss time to provide guidance, reallocate resources, or adjust expectations with their stakeholders. The alternative, hiding problems until they become big issues, erodes trust and creates unnecessary pressure for everyone.

Never any surprises: Your boss hates surprises. Keep them informed about potential risks, changing timelines, or shifting priorities. Even seemingly small changes can have ripple effects throughout an organization that you might not be aware of.

In addition to proactive communication, here are some other important ways to manage up:

Learn their priorities and pressures: Your boss has their own goals, constraints, and people to report to. Understanding their pain points allows you to frame your work in terms that matter to them. I once worked with a brilliant analyst who couldn't understand why his meticulously researched reports weren't appreciated.

He was solving problems nobody asked him to solve. Once he started asking, "What decision does my boss need to make next month?" his work became better.

Make their job easier: The universal currency in all organizations is making someone else's life better. Look for opportunities to lighten your manager's load. This might mean handling routine tasks independently, preparing background information before meetings, or filtering information so they can focus on truly important decisions.

Build trust through reliability: Nothing builds credibility faster than consistently delivering on commitments. When you say something will be done by Friday, make sure it happens. If circumstances change, communicate proactively about adjustments to scope or timeline. Most trust isn't built through grand gestures but through a hundred small promises kept.

Manage expectations: Be realistic about what you can accomplish and distinguish clearly between committed deliverables and aspirational goals. Humans tend to be optimistic about timeframes but pessimistic about outcomes. Reverse this tendency: be conservative about when things will happen, but confident in your ability to deliver quality.

Navigating difficult situations: Even the best manager-employee relationships face challenges. Here's how to handle common difficult scenarios:

» **When you need resources:** Frame requests in terms of organizational goals rather than personal preferences. "To meet the quarterly target, we need additional design support" is more compelling than "I'm feeling overwhelmed and need help."

» **When you make a mistake:** The difference between

a good relationship and a poor one isn't the absence of mistakes. It's how they are handled. Own it completely, explain briefly what happened, present your plan to fix it, and share what you've learned so that it doesn't happen again. Most bosses appreciate accountability more than perfection.

» **When you disagree with a decision:** Choose your battles carefully. For minor issues, sometimes it's best to "disagree and commit." For more significant concerns, present alternative viewpoints respectfully, backed by data when possible. Focus on shared goals rather than personal opinions.

The ultimate goal: a true partnership: The manager-employee relationship might be the most important dynamic in any organization. Your day-to-day experience at work, your opportunities, and your growth all flow through this relationship. When you get good at managing up, you stop seeing your boss as an obstacle to work around and start seeing them as a partner in getting things done. That shift changes everything about how you show up at work. And over time, you become the kind of person others actively want to work with and follow.

A MAGNET FOR TALENT

When Microsoft needed to build Azure, they faced a brutal challenge: create a cloud platform that could compete with Amazon Web Services while most of the company still thought the future belonged to desktop software. Steve Ballmer (then Microsoft's CEO) knew they needed someone exceptional, so they hired Dave Cutler, the legendary engineer behind Windows NT. Ballmer told the story to *Acquired* podcast hosts Ben Gilbert and David Rosenthal: *"And then Cutler brings some of his, I'll call Gang, his favorite guys. He brings them over because he's a magnet for talent and we get started."*

Ballmer knew he wasn't just hiring one engineer. He was hiring a team. Cutler brought with him a network of people who had worked with him before, who trusted his judgment, and who knew that following him usually led to building something important. This is how magnetic leaders work. They don't just change jobs; they bring entire teams of exceptional people who have learned that betting their careers on this person's vision typically pays off.

Every strong professional relationship you build becomes an investment that appreciates over time. The colleague who respects your work today might become the hiring manager who calls you about an opportunity tomorrow. The person you collaborate with effectively could become the executive who brings you into their startup years later. This compounds over time. One person who trusts your judgment can influence ten hiring decisions over their career. Those ten people can influence a hundred. The math works in your favor, but only if you consistently deliver and treat people well along the way. When talented people choose to follow you to new opportunities, it sends a message to everyone else. It suggests you're worth betting on. This creates a cycle where quality attracts more quality. Cutler's team followed him because they had evidence of what working with him was like. They knew the caliber of problems they would solve and the standards they would be held to. That track record became more persuasive than any job posting or compensation package.

Magnetic leadership is built through how you handle the small moments that reveal character. How you respond to disagreements when everyone is stressed. Whether you share credit when projects succeed. How you react when things don't go as planned. People remember these details. They notice whether you support your team during layoffs. They watch how you treat people who can't help your career. These moments accumulate into a reputation that determines whether people will follow you into uncertain situations.

Building this magnetic quality requires thinking in decades, not quarters. You invest in long-term relationships. You prioritize team success over personal recognition. You maintain standards even when it's inconvenient. This patience creates advantages that others can't easily copy. While most people optimize for immediate results, magnetic leaders optimize for long-term trust and consistent value delivery. The difference compounds over time. Being able to attract talent becomes more valuable as your career progresses. Each successful project, each strong relationship, each demonstration of reliable leadership adds to a reputation that opens doors you couldn't access alone.

When companies face their biggest challenges, they don't just want individual contributors. They want people who can attract and work with other exceptional people. That's the difference between being hired for your skills and being hired for the talent upgrade you represent to the entire organization. Becoming a magnet for talent isn't about charisma or office politics. It's about consistently delivering results, treating people well, and building trust through reliable behavior over many years. For those willing to make this investment, it creates the kind of career leverage that compounds throughout your professional life and enables you to attack problems that would be impossible to solve alone. The best part? Once you develop this reputation, opportunities start finding you instead of the other way around.

REFLECTION QUESTIONS

- How would you assess your performance in your current role, and what specific evidence do you have that you're truly excellent at what you do right now?
- What skills does your dream job require that you don't currently have, and what are you personally doing outside of work hours to develop them?
- When you complain about problems in your workplace or community, what specific actions could you take to personally address those issues rather than waiting for others to fix them?
- What would change in your approach to work if you stopped depending on your current company, boss, or industry staying exactly the same forever?
- If you had to commit completely to one career path for the next five years with no backup plan, which path would you choose and why are you not already fully committed to it?
- What work could you create or contribute that would be so valuable that the people you want to connect with would seek you out rather than you having to chase them?
- How do you currently communicate with your manager when things go wrong, and what patterns do you notice in how they respond to unexpected problems versus expected updates?

Take Action

- **Be excellent at your current role.** Before thinking about a promotion, master what's in front of you. Paint those warehouse walls perfectly. Get the groceries exactly right. Excellence in small things creates credibility for bigger things.

- **Develop next-level skills on your own time.** Want to be a better communicator? Write every morning before work. Want to be a better speaker? Take improv classes on weekends. The market rewards valuable skills.

- **Create more value than you extract.** Become a "surplus value" employee who makes promotion a rational business decision.

- **Don't wait for permission to take responsibility.** When you see a problem, fix it before being asked. The most valuable people spot issues before they become crises and solve them without requiring authorization.

- **Build wings.** Develop capabilities that create value regardless of circumstances. Assume change is inevitable and prepare by becoming adaptable rather than trying to make current circumstances permanent.

- **Commit fully.** Stop hedging your bets and keeping one foot out the door. Pick something meaningful and throw yourself completely into it. Big achievements require complete commitment.

- **Make something so good people can't ignore it.** Instead of networking your way to opportunities, create work that makes the right people come to you. Great work is the best networking tool you'll ever have.

- **Master the art of managing up.** Share good news often, bad news early, and never surprise your boss. Learn their working style, understand their pressures, and consistently make their job easier.

- **Take ownership.** When you find yourself saying, "someone should fix this," replace that idea with "How can I make this better?" Move from critic to creator, from passive observer to active participant.

- **Become a magnet for talent.** Build relationships so strong that when you move to new opportunities, exceptional people want to follow you. Treat people well, share credit, and maintain standards even when it's inconvenient.

8

Gaining Perspective

Reflection and Intention

THE POWER OF A "JUST CAUSE"

There is a difference between being busy and doing something that matters. Most people are busy, but few are guided by something deeper. That deeper thing, what Simon Sinek calls a "just cause," is what separates a company people work for from one they truly believe in. It's a vision of the future that is worth struggling for, worth being misunderstood for, worth waking up early and staying late for.

I was reminded of this while recording an episode of *The Learning Leader Show* in Atlanta with Bert Bean (CEO) and Sam Kaufman (CRO) from Insight Global. Insight Global is one of the biggest staffing and professional services firms in the world. We were in Bert's office. He said something that has stayed with me: a *just cause* is a vision of a future state that doesn't yet exist. Its purpose so inspiring and compelling that people are willing to sacrifice and contribute to making it a reality. It's about advancing something meaningful that extends beyond our lifetimes.

The key characteristics of a just cause:

1. It's for something (positive and affirmative).
2. It's inclusive (open to all who wish to contribute).
3. It's service-oriented (benefiting others beyond yourself).
4. It's resilient (able to endure political, technological, and cultural change).
5. It's idealistic (big, bold, and ultimately unachievable).

Unlike finite goals that can be "won," a *just cause* is an ongoing pursuit that inspires continuous improvement and adaptation. Organizations with a clear *just cause* tend to be more resilient, innovative, and capable of inspiring true loyalty from both employees and customers. Bert told us that Insight Global's *just cause* is to "be the light" for the world around them. It comes from scripture, but it is not just about faith. It's about how they want to lead, how they treat people, how they serve their team and customers, and how they build a company that makes an impact beyond the bottom line.

"Be the light" will not show up in a spreadsheet (but you will see it tattooed on Bert's forearm). You can't measure it easily, but in a world where so much can seem temporary and transactional, this kind of clarity has power. It reminds people that their work matters, that their effort contributes to something meaningful, that they are part of a story bigger than themselves. You can run a business without a *just cause*. But it is hard to build something lasting without one. The leaders and organizations we admire most stand for something. They make people feel something. And they do it consistently, not just when it is easy. That kind of leadership is rare, which is exactly why it matters. This is where intention meets reflection. You choose what matters. Then you check, honestly and often, whether your actions made that choice.

This deeper sense of purpose transforms how we make decisions, including the small daily choices that compound over time. When we're anchored to something meaningful, we begin to evaluate our actions not just by immediate results, but by their long-term alignment with what truly matters.

In 1665, the Great Plague shut down London and accidently created one of history's most productive sabbaticals. Isaac Newton, twenty-three years old and recently graduated, had nowhere to go but his family's farm in Woolsthorpe. Forced away from the busyness of academic life, Newton spent eighteen months in what we'd now call deep work. He developed the foundation for calculus, figured out how light works, and laid the groundwork for his theory of gravity. The plague gave Newton uninterrupted time to think and experiment.

We know reflection is valuable, yet most of us still avoid it most days. The challenge is creating the conditions that make deep thinking possible in our noisy, distraction-filled homes and offices. The world has evolved to reward immediate action over contemplation. The online algorithm is optimized for noise over signal. The average person consumes 174 newspapers' worth of information every day, more data than reached someone in the 1800s during their entire lifetime. That's like trying to drink from a firehose while someone asks you to describe the taste of each individual water droplet. The result? We're drowning in information but starving for wisdom. I learned this lesson the hard way. For years, I started each day checking email, news, and social media, telling myself I was "staying informed." Really, I was just feeding my brain a bunch of garbage. It was like starting every morning with a dozen donuts.

Now I like to begin each day reading a long-form essay or chapter from a book followed by twenty to thirty minutes of writing. Sometimes it's a "homework for life" style of journaling my days and key learnings. Other times it's working on an essay to publish on Substack. It's mostly about getting the thoughts out of my head and onto the page. This small change has had compound effects on my thinking and decision-making. It's helped me become clearer about what I believe. Six months before I submitted this book proposal, I started writing at least one hundred words (for it) every morning. Some days it was one hundred. Some days more. Most of it wasn't great. After a month, I had rough material. After three months, I had more than 18,000 words. Only some of it was usable, but that didn't matter. I could see which ideas kept showing up and which ones disappeared. The patterns revealed what actually mattered. Editing became easier because I had options. Bad drafts beat blank pages all day. One hundred words a day became a proposal. The proposal became a book deal with HarperCollins. None of it happens if I wait around for inspiration to strike.

The beauty of reflection is that it costs nothing but time and attention. Yet its benefits accumulate dramatically over years and decades. Creating space for reflection demands the discipline to filter out distractions that masquerade as important work.

Developing the discipline of focus and reflection doesn't happen automatically. Often, we're distracted by something that is urgent but not important. Telling the difference between these two things can be hard. That's why understanding what to eliminate from your focus is so powerful.

Racehorses can teach a lesson about focus. Horses see almost everything. Their eyes sit on the sides of their heads, giving them nearly 360-degree vision. Perfect for spotting predators in the wild. Not as helpful on the racetrack, where that wide vision becomes a liability. A flash in the grandstand, the stride of another horse . . . The smallest distraction can pull them off rhythm and waste speed. Some racehorses are fitted with small leather cups called blinkers to narrow their view, so the horse sees the track ahead and nothing else. The result is straighter lines, steadier pace, faster runs. Blinkers are a simple tool that turns raw instinct into performance.

This lesson travels well beyond horse racing. The most impactful people in any field share a useful trait: they've figured out what to ignore. More information feels like it should lead to better decisions. But that's not always true.

Look at investing. Academic studies show that people who check their portfolios frequently make more trades and earn worse returns than those who check less often. There's an old Wall Street legend about the best-performing accounts belonging to investors who forgot their passwords. While everyone else refreshed their screens obsessively, these accidental long-term holders just let time do its work. The best investors know this. They build systems that automate contributions. They think in decades while others panic over daily moves. It sounds backward, but it's true: in a world drowning in data, the superpower isn't processing more information faster. It's knowing what to tune out. Sometimes the most important thing you can learn is what not to look at.

Focus is about getting better at ignoring what doesn't matter. Every second, your brain is making thousands of tiny decisions about what deserves attention and what gets filtered out. It has to. The alternative would be sensory overload and paralysis. But the problem is that most people never take conscious control of this process. When you don't actively choose what to ignore, your environment chooses for you. The loudest voice wins. The most urgent task gets priority, even if it's not important. You end up living in reaction mode, bouncing from one distraction to the next like a pinball.

Try this tonight: write down what you did today, hour by hour. Include everything, the productive work, the mindless scrolling, the meetings that could have been emails. Put an X through anything that added zero value. Underline things that were somewhat useful but maybe got too much time. Circle the work that actually moved you forward. Now look at the ratio. Most people discover they're spending 80 percent of their time on activities that create 20 percent of their results. The math can be brutal but revealing.

Do this exercise for a week. You'll start to see patterns you never noticed. More importantly, you'll start making different choices, not because you suddenly developed superhuman willpower, but because you finally have data on how you actually spend your days versus how you *think* you spend them.

But even perfect focus has a trap. You can become so good at filtering distractions that you lose sight of why filtering matters in the first place. Efficiency without direction is pointless. The most focused people are anchored to something bigger than optimization for its own sake. They have a reason for their focus that extends beyond personal productivity. That's what transforms discipline from a burden into a natural expression of what they value most. Focus is about doing more of what matters, less of what doesn't, and having a clear reason for the difference. Blinkers are a simple tool that turns raw instinct into performance. The difference with people is that we have to figure out what our blinkers should be. The horse doesn't choose. We do. And that means looking back at what's actually been stealing our attention, then deciding what deserves it going forward.

WOULD YOUR FUTURE SELF THANK YOU?

Even though some mornings I don't feel like it, I've started thinking about decisions through a simple but powerful filter: *"Would my future self thank me for this?"*

Some choices are pure investments: we accept present difficulty for future rewards. Every morning when I go to the gym, I'm essentially telling my future self: "I'm willing to inflict some discomfort on these muscles so you can be healthier as you age." When I spend an evening reading instead of watching Netflix, I'm trading immediate comfort for long-term knowledge. These investment decisions often require willpower because they feel more challenging in the moment. The resistance is real, and pushing through it is part of the process.

But there's another category entirely: alignment decisions. These feel right both now and later. Putting down my phone to deeply listen to my daughter talk about her day. Following my curiosity down a Wikipedia rabbit hole. Helping a neighbor carry heavy things. The satisfaction is immediate, and the long-term benefits (stronger relationships, broader knowledge, community connections) compound naturally.

I used to think good decision-making was mostly about delayed gratification: choosing the hard thing now for the easy life later. But that misses something crucial. The best decisions aren't always sacrifices for the future. When I choose to walk instead of drive, I get immediate benefits: fresh air, movement, time to think. When we cook dinner instead of ordering takeout, we enjoy the process of creating something as a family. When I write in my journal, the act itself clarifies my thinking before any long-term benefits kick in.

The real skill is developing a more sophisticated understanding of time: recognizing that our present and future selves aren't separate entities in competition, but different aspects of the same ongoing experience. This perspective shift has been helpful. Instead of constantly battling between what I want now versus what's good for me later, I start looking for choices that serve both. Instead of viewing my future self as someone I owe something to, I see decisions as ways to create unity across time.

The morning alarm that started this reflection? I got up, read a little bit, wrote, went to the gym, and felt the juice for the entire day. My future self definitely thanked me for that, but so did my present self, immediately. Sometimes the best question to ask yourself is whether the person you're becoming through each small choice is someone you want to be. That question applies to what you do today. But it also applies to what you do with yesterday. The choices you make about the future shape who you become. So do the choices you make about the past. Not what happened to you. Which parts of what happened you decide to carry forward.

REJECTION → GRATITUDE

A young Adam Sandler once sat at a bar with his acting teacher. The teacher, believing he was doing his student a favor, bought him a beer and delivered what he thought was career-saving advice: *"You have heart, but you don't have the talent to be in this business. You should do something else."*

Years later, Sandler was at the peak of his career, one of the most in demand actors in the world. He was out with friends when he spotted that same teacher. Here was a perfect moment for *revenge served cold*, the kind of vindication that people fantasize about, where you get to prove someone's devastating prediction about your future embarrassingly wrong.

But something different happened.

Sandler introduced the teacher to his friends with this simple line: *"This was the only acting teacher in my life nice enough to buy me a beer."*

Adam Sandler took a memory that contained both kindness and harsh feedback, and he chose to focus on the kindness behind the teacher's candor. That's not to say you should pretend that bad things didn't happen, or that they didn't sting. My point is this: you can decide which parts of your story you carry forward. Every time you recall something, you're not just replaying it. You're rebuilding it. And each time you rebuild, you get to choose which parts to reinforce. Adam Sandler's approach is useful for two reasons.

First, resentment is expensive. Carrying anger is like paying compound interest on old debts. It drains resources you could use for better things. Proving people wrong might feel satisfying at first but that fades fast. Eventually you run out of doubters, and you're left wondering what you're actually working for.

Second, forgiveness isn't just good karma, it's good business. Like most careers, entertainment careers are built on repeat collaborations. The person known for grace under pressure gets called back; the one who holds grudges gets quietly dropped from contact lists.

The irony is that the teacher's prediction was probably right at the time. Most people who want to be actors don't make it. The teacher had seen hundreds of hopefuls come and go. His advice was logical based on past patterns. But Adam Sandler understood something the teacher didn't: an impactful career often has less to do with initial talent and more to do with how you handle the inevitable stream of people telling you to quit. Sandler's gratitude fueled his persistence. It kept him working when others stopped. It made him pleasant to be around when others grew bitter. It transformed every setback into a lesson about how to treat people better. The teacher saw someone without enough talent to succeed. What he missed was someone with enough character to outlast the rejections.

WORK WITH GUSTO

David Ogilvy built one of the most impactful advertising agencies in history. He created campaigns that are still studied decades later and helped turn copywriting into an art form. But one of his most lasting lessons had nothing to do with clever headlines or market research.

He has said that he admired people who worked with *gusto.* If you did not enjoy what you were doing, he believed you should find something else. He often quoted a Scottish proverb: *"Be happy while you're living, for you're a long time dead."*

A lot of people think about work in terms of short-term trade-offs. Take a job because it pays well. Stay in a role that drains you because change feels risky. Endure the misery now because it might lead somewhere better later. That thinking turns a career into a video game, where the early levels exist only to unlock the later ones. But real life doesn't work that way.

It's important to recognize that careers have stages. Early on, you are not owed a dream job. You are entering a system where you need to prove yourself, build skills, and earn trust. That usually means starting at the bottom and doing work that feels small. That is not failure. That is training. In those early years, the smartest strategy is to treat every task as a chance to demonstrate excellence. Be the person who raises the standard even in roles others dismiss as unimportant. Those habits compound into credibility and opportunity.

Later in your career, when you have more experience and more options, the equation changes. You (should) have more control over where you work and who you work with. At that point, staying in a soul-crushing role for years is not a sign of toughness. It shows that you are ignoring what matters. If you spend eight hours a day doing work you despise, that is not just eight bad hours. It spills into everything else. It shapes how you treat your family, how you sleep, and how you feel about Monday while you are trying to enjoy Sunday. The misery compounds.

The stepping-stone logic, the idea that hating your job now will lead to something better later, ignores a basic truth about careers. A fancy title is worthless if it costs you your energy, curiosity, and relationships along the way. A VP badge at a random company might impress people on LinkedIn, but it means nothing if you are burned out and bitter. I know because I had one of those jobs. Big title, good money, the company looked good on my résumé. But I had a boss I didn't respect (for a host of reasons) and I dreaded most hours of the working day. It got so bad even my dad noticed that I was short-tempered and irritable. My immediate family (wife and children) definitely felt it. In the end, it wasn't worth it, and I created a plan to move on.

Contrast that with someone who genuinely enjoys what they do. They wake up with energy instead of dread. They approach problems with curiosity instead of resignation. People want to work with them. Those relationships create opportunities that no one can plan in advance.

This is what Ogilvy understood. Enthusiasm compounds the same way money does. A small amount, repeated daily, becomes something big over time, not just in terms of career success but of who you become. People chasing titles often miss this completely. They are so focused on the next rung of the ladder that they neglect the skills, relationships, and reputation that come from showing up with energy right now. They end up with impressive résumés and empty careers.

The Scottish proverb Ogilvy loved gets at the heart of this. We tell ourselves we will be happy later. After the promotion. After the bonus. After we have climbed high enough. But later has a way of never arriving. Meanwhile, we spend the bulk of our waking hours in quiet frustration, hoping a future version of ourselves will finally enjoy life.

Does this mean you should quit your job tomorrow if you hate it? No. Most people can't do that, and rash decisions often backfire. But it does mean that chronic work misery is a luxury you cannot afford. It is irrational when you account for all the hidden costs.

The people who work with gusto are more creative, more resilient, and more pleasant to be around. They make better decisions. Over time, these advantages compound into something that looks like luck, but it is really the natural result of showing up with energy instead of exhaustion. Time is the one asset you cannot earn more of. How you spend it doesn't just determine your bank account. It's who you become and the life you actually live, not the one you plan to live someday. The challenge, of course, is that the path to work that energizes you is not the same for everyone. What drives one person to peak performance might completely derail another. That brings us to an insight worth exploring: the only way to figure it out is by reflecting honestly and consistently on what fuels you and what drains you.

EVERYONE'S MEDICINE IS DIFFERENT

"It's my medicine, dawg," was the response from one of my best receivers when I played quarterback in The Arena Football League for the Birmingham Steeldogs. I saw that he was smoking a blunt outside of the team bus as we got ready to load up to go to the arena for one of our games on the road in Macon, Georgia. Surprised, I said, "Really? That gets you ready to play?" He said, "Yeah, man, this is what I need."

It got me thinking about the fact that we all have our own ways to prepare for big moments. Some people smoke weed; others review the playbook and visualize what they intend to do. I preferred some quiet time to myself to visualize our game plan and focus on my role as the quarterback. Two athletes with two completely different approaches to finding our optimal state. Here's the thing about performance: what works for you might not work for me, and what helps me might not be useful for you. This is one of those simple truths that's easy to acknowledge but hard to internalize.

When it comes to mental preparation, focus, or performance, we often, wrongly, seek universal solutions. The research suggests another approach. Psychologist Yuri Hanin developed a concept called "individual zones of optimal functioning" after studying Olympic athletes for decades. His conclusion was simple but useful: each person has their own emotional and physiological sweet spot for peak performance.

Some athletes perform best when they're amped up and nervous. Others need to be calm and centered. The same level of arousal that makes one person sharp makes another person choke. My receiver had found his zone through weed. For me, it was practice reps, visualization, and solitude. Neither approach was inherently right or wrong, they were just right or wrong for each of us.

The market for performance advice is massive. Books, courses, and coaches all promise the secret formula. But most of these formulas conflict with each other:

- "Wake up at five in the morning."
- "Prioritize sleep over early rising."
- "Do your hardest task first."
- "Start with small wins to build momentum."

What if they're all right, just for different people?

When I reflect on my playing days, I see this pattern everywhere. Everybody had their own unique way to get ready. They all worked. Just not for everyone. We crave certainty and clear instructions. It's uncomfortable to admit that we have to figure out our own recipe through trial and error. But that's exactly what peak performance requires. Think about these variations:

Physical Triggers: Some people need to push their bodies to clear their minds (my approach). Others need physical rest to perform mentally. Some need to eat before a big event; others perform better fasting.

Mental Approaches: Visualization works wonders for some. Others get in their heads if they think too much about what's coming. Some need detailed plans; others perform better with room for improvisation.

Social Dynamics: Certain people draw energy from the crowd and teammates. Others (like many quarterbacks

I've known) need moments of isolation to get centered. The problem isn't finding what works. It's accepting that what works for you might seem crazy to someone else.

There's an important distinction here: Just because something feels good doesn't mean it's helping. My receiver genuinely believed marijuana improved his game. Maybe it did. Maybe it didn't. The truth is complicated. Some "medicines" are actually performance-reducing habits wrapped in comfortable familiarity. Others truly unlock our potential. Telling the difference requires brutal honesty. I've seen players depend on energy drinks that probably hurt more than helped (their hearts would be beating out of their chest in pre-game warm-ups, and they would have the inevitable crash during the actual game). I've watched pre-game rituals that were more superstition than science. And I've witnessed genuinely effective but unconventional approaches get dismissed as weird or unprofessional. The only test that matters is whether it works for you.

FINDING YOUR MEDICINE

So how do you find your personal medicine? It starts with self-awareness:

1. Pay attention to your best performances. What were the conditions? How did you prepare? What was your mental state?
2. Experiment consciously. Change one variable at a time and track the results. Be methodical.

3. Ignore conventional wisdom when necessary. Standard advice is designed for average results, not your peak.
4. Be honest about results. Focus on actual performance, not just how you felt.

In my football career, I learned I performed best when I felt overly prepared (very similar to how I feel today about keynote speeches. Lots of practice reps are my friend). Both physically and mentally. I took every rep in practice. And I liked watching extra films of both my practice reps as well as our upcoming opponents. It helped me to understand their tendencies so I could prepare to exploit them when it was game time. That's what worked for me. That doesn't mean it's right for others. The point is that each person needs to do the work to figure out what it is for them.

This understanding that each person's path to peak performance is unique brings us full circle to the central theme of gaining perspective. Whether it's Newton's forced solitude or my receiver's unconventional preparation, the common thread is the commitment to stepping back and understanding what truly works. You need to have the courage to follow that path even when it differs from conventional wisdom. The discipline of reflection is about creating space to discover who you are, what drives you, and how you can contribute most meaningfully to the world. It's about filtering out the noise to focus on what matters, anchoring your efforts to a purpose larger than yourself, and having honesty to find your own unique formula for peak performance.

In a world that rewards immediate action over careful contemplation, the ability to gain perspective becomes a competitive advantage. But more than that, it becomes the foundation for a well-lived life, one where your daily actions align with your deepest values, where your work energizes rather than drains you, and where you're investing in one of the only assets that truly matters: yourself. The plague that forced Newton into solitude was a crisis. But he turned that crisis into opportunity by maintaining the discipline of reflection. We don't need a plague to create our own periods of productive solitude (although we got some practice at that a few years ago). We just need wisdom to recognize that in a noisy world, the ability to think deeply and gain perspective isn't a luxury. It's essential.

REFLECTION QUESTIONS

- When was the last time you had thirty minutes of complete silence with no phone, no distractions, just you and your thoughts? What does your answer tell you about your relationship with reflection?
- What would you discover about your daily habits if you tracked them honestly for a week? How much time are you spending on activities that create little to no value versus work that actually moves you forward?
- Looking at your worst memories, what are you choosing to remember? Your memory is an editor, not a camera. What story are you choosing to tell yourself?
- Does your work energize you or drain you? If you dread Monday while trying to enjoy Sunday, what does that cost you beyond just eight bad hours a day?
- What is your *just cause*, the vision of the future that's worth struggling for, worth being misunderstood for, worth the sacrifice? Or are you just busy without a deeper purpose?
- When you make decisions, are you asking, "What does my future self need?" or just reacting to what feels good right now? How often do those two align?

- What's your personal "medicine" for peak performance? Have you figured out what actually works for you, or are you following advice that works for other people but might be right for you?

Take Action

- **Create forced reflection time.** Block thirty minutes every morning for writing and/or thinking with zero distractions. No phone, no email, no exceptions. Use this time to process what's happening in your life, not just react to it.
- **Audit your attention ruthlessly.** Track what you do hour by hour for one week. Put an X through anything that added zero value, underline things that got too much time, circle work that actually moved you forward. The ratio might be brutal, but I'll bet it's helpful.
- **Define your Just Cause.** Write down the vision of the future you're working toward that extends beyond your lifetime. Make it positive, service-oriented, and big enough that you can't achieve it alone. Let this guide your daily decisions.
- **Build blinders for what matters.** Identify the three most important things you're working on this year. Then list everything you need to stop paying attention to in order to focus on those three things. Ignoring the rest is an intentional strategy, not a weakness.
- **Ask your future self questions daily.** Before making any significant decision today, pause and ask: "Would my future self thank me for this choice?" Start with small decisions, then apply it to bigger choices.
- **Experiment to find your medicine.** Pick one area where you want to perform better and try different preparation methods over the next month. Track what actually improves your performance versus what just feels comfortable.
- **Practice productive solitude.** Schedule one hour this week to sit alone with no agenda other than thinking. No podcast,

no book, no distraction. Just process what's been happening in your life and what you want to happen next.

- **Evaluate your work honestly.** If your job drains more energy than it gives, create a specific plan to change that within twelve months. Life is too short to spend forty-plus hours a week doing work that makes you miserable.

- **Build self-mastery every day.** Pick one small area where you lack self-control and practice every day for thirty days. Master yourself in small things before trying to master anything else.

9

The Teacher's Path

Mastery Through Mentorship

When you're eight years old, mail is mostly boring: bills for your parents, advertisements for things you don't understand. Then one day, there's an envelope with your name on it. The return address says, "Florida State University." Inside is a handwritten letter on official letterhead. This happened to me. The writer told stories about watching me play football and said he hoped I'd one day be "scoring touchdowns in Doak Campbell Stadium." I was shocked. Someone from Florida State was paying attention to me? At eight years old? Kids believe anything. That can be a good thing.

The letter wasn't from Florida State's coaching staff. It was from Rex Caswell, a family friend who happened to love the Seminoles. He'd donated some money to the program and attended games, but he had no official role.

He was just a fan, originally from Florida, who hoped I might play for his team someday. But that wasn't really why he wrote the letter. Rex wrote it to expand my view of what was possible. To make me believe I was good enough for the number one team in the nation. Florida State was competing for national titles every year back then. The idea that I could play there was crazy.

Sometimes you need someone to push you toward the absurd. Great mentors do this instinctively. They see something in you that you can't see yourself. They believe first, before you have reason to. They root for you when winning seems unlikely. Rex stayed close to our family as I grew up. It turned out I wasn't good enough for Florida State. But I was good enough for other schools, and football paid for my college education.

When my playing days ended, my phone rang.

"Ryan, I've been watching you lead people since you were a kid. I want you to be one of my managers someday. Come work for me as an entry-level sales rep and work your way up."

Rex was a VP of sales at LexisNexis. I had never sold anything in my life. But he believed in me. Again.

I said yes.

That's how my career started. I would go on to earn a few Circle of Excellence awards. And eventually I got promoted to work directly for Rex. His belief created my belief. His willingness to bet on me made me desperate to prove him right.

When someone takes a chance on you, like really puts their name on the line, something changes. You don't just want to succeed for yourself anymore. You want to vindicate their judgment. That's the hidden power of mentorship. It's not just advice or connections. It's the weight of someone else's confidence in you. Rex remains a mentor to me today. He's still one of my biggest fans, telling people about my podcast and pushing me to think bigger.

Now it's my turn. As we climb to positions of influence, we inherit the responsibility to lift others. To see potential before it's obvious. To believe in people before they have reason to believe in themselves. To write letters that seem to come from places they could never imagine reaching. The best mentors don't just give advice. They give permission to dream bigger than you thought possible.

HOW TO BE A GREAT MENTEE

Most impactful leaders have had mentors throughout their careers. Sometimes they are formal arrangements, other times not. This can make it difficult to outline exactly what happens in these conversations, because everyone has a different style and approach.

Building an excellent career is not an individual sport. Even highly individualized pursuits like writing books or playing tennis are rarely (if ever) accomplished with one person's effort. Dig into someone's story and you will find that along the way they received guidance and developed relationships with people who shared wisdom or directly became a part of their life. I love reading the acknowledgments in books. Typically, there are lots of people the author thanks because, without them, the book wouldn't have happened.

This is why the most impactful leaders often turn around and do the same for others. They go out of their way to mentor people because they were mentored themselves. It can be intimidating to ask someone for help, especially someone you admire. But it's worth it. Here are some things to remember when positioning yourself to be someone else's mentee:

1. **Be specific. Avoid "picking their brain."** Most people approach mentorship backward. They schedule a coffee and say, "I'd love to pick your brain." I do not like that phrase. It sounds gross and it's so lazy. It shows that you haven't done any work. I'm not saying it's a deal-breaker (I try to have grace for people earlier in their career, because I made those mistakes too), but it doesn't help.

   Smart mentees do the opposite. Before meeting with a mentor, they send a brief outline of exactly what they want to discuss. Not vague topics, but specific challenges they're facing and precise questions they want answered. "I'm struggling with how to prioritize competing projects when everything feels urgent. How do you decide what gets your attention first when you have five things that all matter?"

   This does something powerful. It shows the mentor you've already invested time thinking about the problem. It gives them something concrete to think about. It helps them be a better mentor. And it makes them feel genuinely helpful rather than like a random advice dispenser.
2. **Listen and respond.** During the conversation, the best mentees do a few things well: they ask their prepared questions, they *listen*, ask follow-ups, and they take

notes. Note-taking isn't just about remembering information. It's a visual signal that what the other person is saying matters enough to preserve.

During the conversation, stay focused on what your mentor is saying and respond in kind like you would a peer or someone you care about. Do not use the interaction for some transactional ulterior motive. Stay open to where the conversation may naturally go.

3. **Follow up.** Within a day, great mentees send a follow-up email. Not just "Thanks for your time." Something substantive. They summarize what they learned, and they outline the specific actions they plan to take based on the conversation. *There are talkers and doers. Be a doer.* "You mentioned that successful prioritization starts with identifying what only I can do. This week, I'm going to audit my current projects and delegate the three tasks that someone else could handle just as well."

Then, at the end of the email, they write: "I know you mentor other people beyond me. Feel free to forward this to anyone you think it might help."

This ending transforms the relationship. Suddenly, you're not just another person seeking advice. You're a multiplier of their impact. You've documented their thoughts in a shareable format and given them an easy way to help others. You've turned your mentorship session into content they can use to mentor others without additional effort. Most mentors work with multiple mentees. Most mentees send generic thank-you notes if they send anything at all. The ones who document learnings, commit to action, and offer to amplify the mentor's impact stand out.

I started doing this early in my career without any grand plan. Mainly as a way to document my learnings and to try to add some value to my mentors. I wanted them to want to say yes when I asked to meet with them. Years later, a longtime mentor I originally met on a Circle of Excellence awards trip, named Lee Rivas, called encouraging me to apply for a VP of sales role that reported to him. During our conversation, he mentioned those follow-up emails. They had shown him something about how I operated: I took advice seriously, I followed through on commitments, and I thought about how to create value for others.

The best mentorships are transformational. They change both the mentor and mentee. The mentor feels useful, the mentee gets better guidance, and both benefit from a relationship built on demonstrated respect for each other's time and expertise.

The formula is simple: prepare specific questions, listen actively, ask more questions, take notes, follow up with key learnings and commitments, and offer to multiply their impact. Do this consistently, and you'll become their favorite mentee. People remember how you made them feel. And nothing makes a mentor feel better than knowing their advice didn't just get heard but actually changed how someone operates in the world.

THE CYCLE

The best mentors aren't necessarily the people with the most experience or credentials. They're the ones who remember what it felt like to have someone believe in them before they believed in themselves. This matters because the best mentees eventually become the best mentors.

They carry the memory of being truly seen when they felt invisible.

Rex Caswell taught me this without meaning to. His letter was encouragement. It was also proof that someone was paying attention. And years later when he offered me a job, he wasn't betting on my résumé. He was investing in something he'd recognized in my character long before I'd proven it to anyone else.

This is how mentorship really works. Rather than a hierarchy where wisdom flows downward from experienced to inexperienced, mentorship forms a circle where today's mentees become tomorrow's mentors, carrying forward both knowledge and the spirit of investment in others.

The transition from being mentored to mentoring others requires a deliberate choice. You have to decide to extend the same faith that someone once extended to you. You have to bet on potential rather than proven performance. This explains why the most impactful leaders often turn around and do the same for others. They go out of their way to mentor people because they understand that mentorship is how excellence perpetuates itself. Wisdom gets transferred through these relationships. We honor the people who took chances on us by taking chances on others. The cycle continues only when we choose to keep it alive. So, the question becomes . . . Who are you going to see before they see themselves?

HOW TO BE A GREAT MENTOR

Being asked to mentor someone signals deep trust. It means someone believes you've got not just knowledge, but good judgment. Think of the type of person you would want as a mentor. What types of qualities do they have? What kind of person are they?

Offering yourself up to mentor others not only has the potential to change someone else's life, but it can be a great learning tool for the mentor. This is why I push all of the leaders I work with to put themselves in positions to teach on a regular basis. That's when you really have to know your stuff.

But how do we go about this? What happens when someone asks us to mentor them? How should we approach it?

There are a few key principles to think about.

Breathe Life into Others

People who inspire others understand a fundamental truth about human nature. We don't follow detailed instructions as much as we follow people who make us feel something. This isn't complicated psychology. It's how we're wired. Great leaders inspire others to take action, to work toward a common goal, to do the work that must be done. The word "inspire" means to "breathe life into." It's the opposite of expire. This etymology reveals something profound about what happens when someone truly inspires us. They don't just motivate. They animate us at our core.

History shows that inspiration isn't about authority or credentials. Gandhi had neither when he started. Neither did most people who changed the world. What they had was an authentic connection to something bigger than themselves that others could feel. The most inspiring people I've known share a surprising trait. They ask questions more than they give answers. They're genuinely curious about others. This creates space for people around them to grow into better versions of themselves.

Inspiration differs from motivation in a critical way. Motivation pushes you forward, often through incentives or pressure. Inspiration pulls you forward through the gravity of possibility. One depletes over time. The other compounds.

The true test of whether someone has inspired others isn't what happens when they're in the room. It's what happens when they leave it. Do people continue working toward the shared vision with the same enthusiasm? If yes, that's not just leadership. That's having breathed life into something that now sustains itself.

Be Articulate

In 1961, Richard Feynman stepped into a first-year physics classroom at Caltech. The Nobel laureate wasn't there to make a guest appearance; he had committed to teaching the introductory course himself. There is an old legend about Feynman that says when his colleagues questioned why someone of his stature would "waste time" teaching basics to freshmen, Feynman is supposed to have said, "If you want to master something, teach it." What Feynman discovered through experience, modern science has now confirmed through lots of research: *teaching transforms how we learn and is one of the most powerful learning tools that exists.*

The simple act of organizing information for someone else's consumption forces us to confront our own understanding in ways that passive learning never could. Here are three practical approaches that have emerged from both research and real-world experience:

1. **The "Explain It Tomorrow" Method:** Before diving into any new material, imagine you'll need to teach it to someone else tomorrow. This mental shift activates different learning pathways in your brain. Instead of passively consuming information, you'll automatically begin organizing it in ways that make it teachable. Software development teams often use this principle. When engineers know they'll need to explain their code to others in reviews, they write clearer, better-documented code.
2. **The Documentation Practice:** Write explanations for complex processes as if teaching them to a newcomer. This has become fundamental in the open-source software community, where developers must write clear documentation so others can understand and build upon their work. The process of creating this documentation often reveals gaps in understanding that wouldn't otherwise be apparent.
3. **The Apprentice Model:** Regularly put yourself in teaching situations with various levels of learners. Each level forces you to understand the material differently. This is why many traditions, from woodworking to cooking, have long relied on a master-apprentice model, the process of teaching apprentices helps masters refine and deepen their own understanding.

Consider how this plays out in organizational learning. Toyota's famous "train the trainer" approach demonstrates this. Their production system is built around the idea that every leader must be capable of teaching their work to others. The act of teaching forces leaders to deeply understand every aspect of their processes. The result is a culture where learning and teaching are inseparable from doing. This goes beyond manufacturing. When legendary management consultant Peter Drucker advised executives, he wouldn't give them answers. Instead, he asked questions that forced them to teach him about their business. Through the process of explaining their challenges and operations, executives often discovered solutions themselves.

Here's how leaders can implement this in a practical way:

- Start team meetings by having different members teach new skills or explain recent projects.
- Institute a "weekly wisdom" session where team members take turns teaching their colleagues.
- Create internal documentation as teaching tools, not just reference materials.

Use the Feynman technique in real situations:

- Choose a concept you need to master.
- Explain it to a non-expert.
- Identify gaps in your explanation.
- Return to the source material to fill those gaps.
- Repeat until you can explain it simply.

The key insight from the research is that teaching creates better comprehension than studying alone. Many impactful organizations have implemented this by creating structured opportunities for knowledge sharing and teaching. Some companies have instituted "lunch and learn" sessions where team members teach their colleagues about their areas of expertise. Others have created mentorship programs that benefit both the mentor and mentee through the teaching process. The most effective leaders are perpetual teachers. They understand that their role is to build understanding and capability in others. And in doing so, they deepen their own mastery.

Benjamin Graham, the father of value investing, said that his experience teaching at Columbia Business School didn't just benefit his students (including Warren Buffett), it helped him refine and clarify his own investment principles. The process of teaching forced him to distill complex financial concepts into clear, actionable insights that became the foundation of modern value investing. His classic book *The Intelligent Investor* emerged from this teaching experience, demonstrating how the discipline of teaching others can lead to deeper mastery of your craft.

In an age of increasing complexity, the ability to make the complex simple is essential. Every time a leader invests the time to teach, they're engaging in one of the most powerful forms of personal development available.

Be Honest

University of Houston basketball coach Kelvin Sampson understands the importance of telling the truth: "If you're going to build a culture, the first thing you have to come to grips with, you're going to have confrontation." He goes further: "The coaches that fail at every level are the coaches that are passive aggressive. Passive aggressive coaches are usually afraid to hold kids accountable; they rationalize." This gets at something fundamental about human groups. People don't just respond to incentives. They respond to standards and expectations. And standards without enforcement aren't standards at all. They're suggestions.

I've noticed that a lot of great leaders share a useful trait: they're willing to say the thing that others are scared to bring up. They'll point out when work isn't good enough. They'll have the conversation everyone else avoids. They understand that momentary discomfort prevents long-term disaster. The math of confrontation is helpful to understand. A five-minute difficult conversation today prevents five months of declining performance tomorrow. But our brains aren't wired this way. We overvalue immediate peace and undervalue long-term culture. My friend and teammate, Geron Stokes, has a simple saying about this. ***"See it, say it."*** Meaning, when you see someone doing it great. Tell them. When you see someone not meeting the standard, tell them immediately. *See it, say it*. Don't wait for the quarterly review. Say it right now.

The passive-aggressive leader thinks they're being nice by not confronting underperformance. What they're actually doing is lowering the standard. This isn't kindness. It's selfishness. That person is choosing *their own comfort* instead of doing what's best for the other person and the team. Great organizations feel safe because everyone knows exactly where they stand. There's safety in clarity, even when that clarity isn't what you want to hear.

History shows us that cultures don't decline suddenly. They erode when small infractions go unaddressed, when expectations become fuzzy, when "this is fine" becomes the default response to things that aren't fine at all. The irony is that confrontation, done right, isn't about creating conflict. It's about preventing larger conflicts down the road. It's an investment, with short-term costs and long-term returns. As Coach Sampson suggests, you cannot build anything worthwhile without the willingness to confront problems. The alternative isn't harmony. It's mediocrity disguised as peace. And that's a price no ambitious organization can afford to pay.

Be Observant

There's a story about Maria Montessori that gets to the heart of something we all struggle with: the gap between what we *think* we know and what we *actually* know.

In 1907, Montessori was asked to supervise a daycare in the slums of Rome. She was a physician, not an educator. She had theories about child development, but theories are different from reality. Reality is messier.

So, she did something most experts would never do. She admitted she didn't know what she was doing. Instead of imposing a curriculum, she watched. Instead of teaching, she listened. Instead of lecturing children about how they should behave, she observed how they behaved when left to their own devices. What she discovered changed everything for her.

The children didn't need to be entertained. They wanted to work. Real work. Meaningful work. They concentrated for hours on tasks that adults assumed would be boring. They preferred order to chaos, quiet to noise, reality to fantasy. Every assumption she had about children was wrong. Every assumption most adults had about children was wrong. But here's the thing: she only learned this because she was teaching. You can't discover what children want by reading about children. It's hard to understand human nature from a textbook. You have to do the thing (think about the Robin Williams conversation with Matt Damon on the park bench in *Good Will Hunting*).

The person who teaches often learns more than the person who is taught. Teaching forces you to confront reality. When you're just thinking about something, you can fool yourself. Your mind fills in the gaps. You assume things work the way you think they should work. But when you have to make something work in the real world, with real people, all your assumptions get tested.

Montessori thought she was going to teach children. Instead, children taught her. They taught her that motivation comes from within, not from external rewards. They taught her that children are capable of far more than adults assume.

This isn't unique to education. It happens everywhere.

I've learned this firsthand when it comes to running a business. I went back to school to earn my MBA. I thought I learned a lot about business through the process of earning a graduate degree. Then a few years later, I actually started my own business. That's when you really learn about business. When it's your own money on the line. Your family's livelihood depends on you earning enough money to pay your mortgage, feed your children, save for college, and so on. You want to learn about something? *Do the thing*. There's something about skin in the game that changes everything. When your reputation is on the line, when real people are counting on you, when failure has consequences, you pay attention differently. You notice things you wouldn't otherwise.

Montessori could have spent her entire career reading about child development. She could have written papers about learning theory. She could have attended conferences and given speeches about education. But she would never have developed the Montessori method. The method emerged because she was willing to put herself in a position where children could teach her. She had to surrender her expertise to gain real knowledge.

This can be uncomfortable. Most people like being an expert. We like having the answers. We like being the one who knows. But the people who make the biggest breakthroughs are usually the ones who are willing to be confused, to be wrong, to be taught by the very people they're supposed to be teaching. Montessori's greatest insight wasn't about children. It was about learning itself. Real learning happens when you engage with reality, not when you think about reality from a distance. The children in that Roman slum didn't just learn from Montessori. They taught her something that changed education forever: the best way to learn is to teach, and the best way to teach is to learn.

A LEGENDARY CASE STUDY IN MENTORSHIP

In the 1970s, a young woman approached Maya Angelou after a university speaking engagement. The woman wanted an interview. Angelou politely declined. She was busy, tired, and had said no to countless similar requests. But the young woman persisted with a simple proposition: "If you'll just give me five minutes . . ."

Angelou agreed, expecting the usual rushed questions and superficial answers. Instead, something really cool happened. The young woman asked thoughtful questions, listened carefully to the responses, and asked better follow-up questions. After five minutes, she said thank you and goodbye. Years later, Angelou would recall, "I looked at my watch, and it had been exactly five minutes." She remembered thinking, "I liked that in her."

The young woman was Oprah Winfrey.

What started as a five-minute conversation eventually became a thirty-year friendship that would benefit both women in ways neither could have imagined. But their deep relationship didn't truly develop until 1984, when Angelou spotted Oprah walking down a street in Chicago and decided to say hello. That chance encounter rekindled their connection and launched a mentorship that would shape both of their lives. Angelou became Oprah's "mentor-mother-sister-friend," offering wisdom during the most important years of Oprah's career. In return, Oprah became one of the most powerful amplifiers of Angelou's message, introducing her work to millions through TV, magazines, and personal appearances.

This story reveals something counterintuitive about teaching and mentoring: the person doing the helping often gains as much as the person being helped.

We tend to think of mentorship as a one-way transaction. The experienced person gives knowledge, wisdom, and guidance to someone less experienced. The mentor sacrifices time and energy. The mentee receives value. End of story. But real mentorship works differently. It creates a feedback loop where both parties benefit in unexpected ways.

Maya Angelou found someone who not only appreciated her wisdom but had the platform and influence to share it with the world. Oprah featured Angelou dozens of times on her show, quoted her philosophy in magazines, and continued promoting her work decades after they first met. When Angelou turned seventy, Oprah rented a cruise ship and took 150 people to celebrate among the Mayan ruins. The mentee became the mentor's greatest advocate.

This pattern repeats itself all the time. Teachers learn from explaining concepts to students who ask questions they've never considered. Parents discover new perspectives while helping their children navigate problems. Managers develop better leadership skills by coaching their teams through challenges. Teaching forces you to organize your thoughts, clarify your reasoning, and defend your positions. It reveals gaps in your own knowledge. It pushes you to stay current and think differently. Most importantly, it creates relationships with people who will remember your investment in them.

There's another benefit that's harder to measure but equally important: *meaning*. Angelou once told Oprah, "When you learn, teach. When you get, give." This was insight into how purpose works. The act of helping others creates a sense that your experiences matter, that your struggles weren't in vain, that your knowledge has value beyond your own life. When Oprah spoke about mistakes she had made in her twenties, Angelou responded with words that became one of Oprah's core philosophies: *"When you know better, you do better."* In that moment, Angelou was transforming her own difficult experiences into wisdom that could help someone else. The pain had purpose.

This is why the best mentors aren't always the most successful people. They're the ones who understand that teaching amplifies the value of everything they've learned.

They know that helping others helps them clarify what they actually believe and why it matters.

During Angelou's memorial service in 2014, Oprah said she had learned more from her mentor than from anyone else. But if you study their relationship closely, you'll notice that Angelou seemed to get as much from the friendship as she gave. That five-minute conversation in the 1970s created value that compounded for decades. Both women became better versions of themselves because of their connection to each other.

The lesson isn't that you should mentor people hoping to get something back. It's that genuine teaching and helping others create unexpected returns. When you invest in someone else's success, you often discover that you've invested in yourself. Sometimes the most generous thing you can do is also the most selfish thing you can do. That's not a contradiction. That's just how human relationships work when they work well.

REFLECTION QUESTIONS

- Who is one person in your life who believed in you before you believed in yourself? How did that change what you thought was possible?
- Who in your world might need you to believe in them right now? How could you show them that belief?
- Think about the last time you asked someone for advice. Did you come prepared with specific questions, or did you just "pick their brain"? How could you make the next conversation more meaningful for both of you?
- What advice have you been given that you haven't acted on yet? Why not?
- When was the last time you taught someone something? What did you learn about yourself in the process?

- What is one uncomfortable truth you've been avoiding sharing with someone you lead or mentor? What would happen if you said it kindly and clearly?
- Where might your assumptions about people, processes, or problems be wrong? And how could observing before acting reveal a better path forward?
- If someone followed you around for a week, what would they learn about what you value? Would that match what you want to teach?

Take Action

- **Write a letter to someone's potential.** Find a younger person in your field and send them a handwritten note about what you see in them that they might not see in themselves yet. The best mentors believe in people before there's evidence to support that belief.
- **Become the mentee everyone wants to help.** Before asking for advice, prepare (at least) three specific questions about real challenges you're facing. Take notes during the conversation. Send a follow-up email within a day summarizing what you learned and what actions you're going to commit to.
- **Test your understanding by teaching it.** Pick something you think you know well and try to explain it to someone else.
- **Get comfortable with uncomfortable conversations.** When you see work that doesn't meet standards, address it as soon as possible. Have a *"see it, say it"* mentality for both great work and work that doesn't meet the standard. Leaders who tell the truth with the intention to love and care for someone are leaders others want to follow.
- **Learn something new by agreeing to teach it.** Volunteer to train someone on a skill you want to master yourself. The pressure of having to teach it will force you to understand it better than studying alone ever could.

- **Turn your mistakes into other people's wisdom.** After you screw something up or learn a hard lesson, write down what you discovered. Share it with people who might face similar situations. Your pain can have purpose.

- **Create regular opportunities for people to teach each other.** Host working sessions where team members explain their expertise to colleagues. Most organizations aren't great at internal knowledge sharing. Be the person who fixes that.

- **Challenge your assumptions by actually looking.** Pick one belief you hold about how people behave in your industry, then spend a month watching to see if reality matches your theory. You'll be surprised how often it doesn't.

- **Amplify the people who help you.** When someone invests in your success, find ways to promote their work to your network. The best mentoring relationships create value for both people, not just the person getting advice.

- **Make teaching a habit, not an event.** Commit to explaining one thing you learned this week to someone else. Teaching regularly will make you better at everything you encounter because it forces you to really understand it.

Keep Going

Looking back, I am very fortunate for so many of the leaders who I've worked or played for in my life. But a few of them rise above the rest. Like Coach Terry Hoeppner, who shaped my early career with two simple but powerful practices. The first was his daily reminder (that I shared to open this book): "*Have a plan, work the plan, and plan for the unexpected.*" These words became (and remain) part of my operating system. The second was his ritual of reading poems to our team. One in particular, "Don't Quit" by Edgar Albert Guest, became the foundation of our team's identity. Here is the poem:

When things go wrong, as they sometimes will,
When the road you're trudging seems all uphill,
When the funds are low and the debts are high, and you want to smile but you have to sigh,
When care is pressing you done a bit - rest if you must, but don't you quit.

Life is queer with its twists and turns.
As everyone of us sometimes learns.
And many a fellow turns about, when he might have won had he stuck it out.
Don't give up though the pace seems slow - you may succeed with another blow.
Often the goal is nearer than it seems to a faint and faltering man;
Often the struggler has given up when he might have captured victor's cup;
And he learned too late when the night came down,
How close he was to the golden crown.
Success is failure turned inside out - the silver tint of the clouds of doubt,
And when you never can tell how close you are,
It may be near when it seems afar;
So stick to the fight when you're hardest hit - it's when things seem worst, you must not quit.

The strangest thing about excellence is how boring it looks from the outside. While everyone searches for the secret formula, the breakthrough moment, the life-changing epiphany, the people who actually sustain excellence are usually doing something much less dramatic: they're showing up again and again. They're practicing a lot. They're making small improvements that no one notices. They're choosing the harder right over the easier wrong, one decision at a time.

This is what I've learned after interviewing more than seven hundred leaders and watching the patterns that separate those who sustain excellence from those who don't.

Becoming someone worth following is about the accumulation of small, consistent choices over time. It's about paying a price that most people aren't willing to pay.

The price isn't money. It's comfort. We live in the most comfortable era in human history, yet so many feel unfulfilled and frustrated with their progress. This isn't a coincidence. Comfort and growth exist in tension with each other. The innovations that make life easier also make personal development harder. We can order food on an app, find any answer in seconds, and avoid almost every form of friction that people only a few decades ago faced daily. But friction creates strength. The resistance we try to eliminate is often exactly what we need most. As eight-time Mr. Olympia (bodybuilding) winner Ronnie Coleman said, *"Everybody wanna be a bodybuilder . . . But nobody wanna lift these heavy ass weights!"*

The people I've met who have built something lasting made peace with this early. They understood that the price of becoming excellent is the willingness to be perpetually uncomfortable. Stretched, not miserable. Challenged enough to grow but not so much they break. And they stay hungry even (and especially) when they succeed. Paul Rabil took one hundred shots every day, even when he didn't feel like it. Katherine Johnson questioned every calculation, even when others accepted the answers. Rex Caswell wrote letters to an eight-year-old about possibilities that seemed absurd. None of these actions felt significant in the moment. All of them compounded into something great.

Personal growth follows the same mathematics as compound interest, but the returns are invisible for years. Small actions, repeated consistently, create disproportionate results over time. The tough part? There's a cruel gap between effort and evidence. You can practice for months and feel no different. You can invest in yourself daily and see no progress. The changes are happening beneath the surface, invisible to everyone, including you. This is why most people quit. They're looking for immediate results in a world that rewards consistency and patience. They expect to feel different tomorrow because they worked hard today. But real development doesn't work that way. It's more like building muscle or learning a language . . . The gains accumulate slowly and reveal themselves over time.

The people who become excellent leaders understand this math. They know that consistent daily practice creates exceptional lifetime results. They make investments in themselves that others can't see and wouldn't value if they could. Charlie Munger read a ton for ninety-nine years, because the accumulated knowledge compounded into wisdom that money couldn't buy. Leonardo da Vinci practiced *ostinato rigore* because he understood that relentless precision in small things creates breakthroughs in big things.

The price of becoming isn't paid once. It's paid for daily, in small increments, often when no one is watching. The stories we tell about successful people are almost always focused on the moment they "made it" and ignore the years they spent making themselves ready for that moment. We watch Maggie Rogers go viral in a college classroom and forget the years she spent writing songs alone in her room. We see entrepreneurs "suddenly" break through and miss the failed ventures that taught them everything.

Excellence isn't about being in the right place at the right time. It's about preparing yourself so thoroughly that when opportunity arrives, you're ready to make the most of it. This preparation usually happens in private. It's the hours no one sees. It's like what Muhammad Ali said, "The fight is won or lost far away from witnesses—behind the lines, in the gym, and out there on the road, long before I dance under those lights." There are trade-offs. The most impactful people aren't necessarily more talented. They're more prepared. They've paid the price of becoming excellent before anyone asked them to prove it.

There's something else I've noticed about people who sustain excellence over decades: they become teachers, whether formally or informally. They share what they've learned. They lift others up. They pass on the wisdom they've accumulated. This isn't just to be a nice person. It's enlightened self-interest. Teaching clarifies thinking. Mentoring reveals gaps in knowledge. Helping others forces you to articulate what you actually believe and why it matters. The act of giving away knowledge makes you wiser.

Here's the brutal truth about careers, relationships, and life: everything external can be taken away. The economy can crash. Companies can fail. Industries can disappear overnight. The only investment that can never lose value is the one you make in yourself. Your skills, your judgment, your character, your ability to learn and adapt. These are portable assets that compound over time. They can't be outsourced, automated, or stolen. They're yours as long as you're willing to keep developing them. This is why the most secure people aren't those with the most stable jobs. They're those with the most valuable strengths. They trust their wings, not the branch they're sitting on.

Building these capabilities requires a long-term perspective that's increasingly rare. Most people optimize for the next quarter, the next promotion, the next validation. The most impactful people optimize for the next decade (or longer). They're willing to look foolish in the short term to build something meaningful in the long term. They're comfortable with delayed gratification because they understand that the best things in life come to those who consistently get after it each day and grow slowly.

After studying lots of exceptional careers, I've come to believe that the price of becoming excellent is also its greatest privilege. The sacrifice of immediate pleasure becomes the satisfaction of meaningful achievement. The loneliness of uncommon choices becomes the community of uncommon people. You don't pay this price to get something. You pay it to become someone. Someone who solves problems others can't solve. Someone who creates value for others. Someone who sees possibilities when there is a lot of uncertainty. This transformation isn't guaranteed. You can do everything right and still fail. You can invest in yourself and see no return. But here's what is guaranteed: if you don't go for it, you definitely won't become who you're capable of becoming. If you don't do the work, you won't get the results over the long term.

The choice isn't between success and failure. It's between *becoming* and *staying* the same. It's between growing and settling. It's easier to stay in that planted pot inside. As Mr. Feeny pointed out though, if you stay there, you'll stop growing. In the end, the price of becoming isn't about achieving specific outcomes. It's about the direction of your life. It's about whether you're moving toward who you want to be. It's about whether you're expanding or contracting, learning or stagnating, contributing or consuming.

The most impactful people I know aren't those who achieved all of their goals. They're those who became the kind of people capable of achieving goals they couldn't have imagined when they started. You give yourself permission to pay the price of becoming excellent now. The price is high. The privilege is higher. And the payment plan lasts a lifetime.

But here's the beautiful part: every day you get to choose whether to make another payment or walk away from the investment. Every morning you wake up with the opportunity to become a slightly better version of yourself. Every moment offers the chance to choose growth over comfort, learning over knowing, becoming over being. The price of becoming is never paid in full. But neither is the return. Both compound forever. The question isn't whether you can afford to pay the price. The question is whether you can afford not to.

Acknowledgments

After thousands of conversations, I know this: solo efforts rarely produce the best work. Ideas improve when you borrow them, discuss them, and build with other people. Scott Galloway has told me multiple times, *"Greatness is in the agency of others."* This book exists because generous, brilliant people invested their time in it. Here are some of them . . .

End of the Podcast Club members . . . Listeners of *The Learning Leader Show*: Your feedback is my fuel. It's the juice! Thank you for your continued support and willingness to share your personal stories about how the podcast has helped you. It means more than you realize.

Dave Moldawer: For being there for me in those early days when I battled with the proposal. Your calm demeanor and consistent feedback made this book what it is. Thank you.

Hollis Heimbouch: Your title is SVP/Publisher at HarperCollins . . . but you are so much more than that for me. Thank you for being a trusted adviser/confidant/friend. Thank you for believing in me and this idea, and your constant encouragement to keep going. Especially when I'm texting/emailing you about minor tweaks I want to make at all hours of the day.

Dan Smith: Dude. Thank you for taking a bunch of random ideas and helping me turn them into a book that will change many people's lives. Thank you for caring about every single word in the manuscript. It means a ton to me.

Liam Murray: You're always there to bounce ideas off of. You tell the truth. You aren't afraid. And you're curious and super thoughtful. Thank you.

Sam Kaufman and Bert Bean: So grateful that I get to work with you. Doing big things. Making a huge impact. Leading a company the right way. You guys are the example I share with others about how to be excellent senior leaders at a big company. So cool to see it. Grateful to be part of it.

Rob and Cheri Kimbel: So grateful for your support, guidance, and friendship. You guys are a one of one. I'm inspired by your selfless service and your work to create opportunities to improve lives. You've improved mine! And so many others'. Thank you.

Podcast guests who have become friends/confidants/people for me to talk through the ideas in this book: Brad Stulberg, Liz Wiseman, Susan Cain, Tim Ferriss, Ed Latimore, James Clear, Tom Ryan, Nick Thompson, Dan Coyle, Pat Lencioni, Dave Berke, Derek Sivers, Jake Tapper, David Epstein, Suzy Welch, Morgan Housel, Arthur Brooks, Ryan Petersen, Michelle Curran, Shaka Senghor, Helen Lewis, Tony Reno, Stan McChrystal, Anthony Consigli, Mike Maples Jr, Jenny Wood, Chase Jarvis, Lawrence Yeo, Meg Meeker, George Dubs, Seth Godin, Don Miller, Will Guidara, Kim Campbell, Dan Pink, Michael Easter, Tara Viswanathan, Jason Fried, Paul Rabil, Ryan Holiday, David Perell, Tony Robbins, Scott Galloway, Jim Dethmer, Scott Belsky, Rob Henderson, Ariel Helwani, Bill Ury, Jim Collins, Tim Urban, Dan Patrick, Eric Potterat, Tim Ryan, Shane Parrish, Jack Raines, Jesse Cole, Buzz Williams, Cody Keenan, Todd Henry, Oz Pearlman, Mike Deegan, Brent Beshore, Jimmy Soni, Kat Cole, and many others I'm sure I'm missing.

Learning Leader Team: Brook Cupps, Geron Stokes, Eli Leiker, and (the GOAT) Sherri Coale. Thank you for being the best teammates ever. I am so grateful that I get to do this with you. A team of *get-after-it*, "see it, say it," no-nonsense doers. I love you guys.

My parents (Pistol & Judy Hawk): From day one . . . and consistently every day since. Thank you for your love and support. Always there. I hit the parent lottery. So grateful for you.

My brothers, Matt (Berk) and AJ: Constant and unyielding support. Always there. The ultimate dudes. So grateful for you. Laura: An amazingly loving and supportive sister-in-law. Thank you.

Brooklyn, Ella, Addison, Payton, and Charlie: I love you. So much. And I am very proud of you. Thank you for being you.

Miranda: The only person I know (other than Pistol) to have a 100 percent approval rating. You are loved by all who know you for good reason. Kind, loving, caring, tough, resilient. Always making it happen. I love you.

■ ■ ■

The Price of Becoming builds on research and analysis that went into my first three books, *Welcome to Management*, *The Pursuit of Excellence*, and *The Score That Matters*. Like those books, it appropriates the thoughts of many authorities whose work is credited in the text and citations. It also builds upon the insights gained in conversations, both recently and over decades of my life. I hope it's useful for you.

*"What is beauty? Is beauty a pretty face, a nice smile, flowing hair, nice skin? Not to me, it's not. To me beauty is living life to higher standards, stronger morals, and ethics and believing in them, whether people tell you you're right or wrong. Beauty is not wasting a day. Beauty is noticing life's little intricacies and taking time out of your busy day to really enjoy those little intricacies. Beauty is being real, being genuine, being pure with no facade—what you see is what you get. Beauty is expanding your mind, always seeking knowledge, not being content, always going after something and challenging yourself. I believe that to really honor Pat, we should all challenge ourselves. No more *I'm going to do this* or *I'm going to do that*. Do it. As Pat would say, probably, 'Get off your ass and do it.' Why, you ask, should we honor him this way? Because that's what Pat did his whole life."

—Jake Plummer describing his friend Pat Tillman

Notes

CHAPTER 1:

Contemplate, Copy, Create: Building Skills Through Mindful Imitation

4 *"Imitate, then innovate":* Ryan Hawk, host, *The Learning Leader Show with Ryan Hawk*, episode #579, "How to Cultivate Taste with David Perell," podcast, Insight Global, April 21, 2024, 1 hour, 23 minutes, https://learningleader.com/davidperell579/.

5 *"You'll be the only":* Ryan Hawk, host, *The Learning Leader Show with Ryan Hawk*, episode #619, "Pattern Breakers: Why Some Leaders Change the Future, with Mike Maples Jr.," podcast, Insight Global, January 26, 2025, 1 hour, 6 minutes, https://learningleader.com/mikemaplesjr/.

6 *"if I left it there, it would stop growing": Boy Meets World*, season 1, episode 2, "I Dream of Feeny," written by April Kelly, directed by David Trainer, aired September 30, 1993, on ABC.

9 *"this incomparable artist":* Chalamet, Timothée, "Outstanding Performance by a Male Actor in a

Leading Role acceptance speech," The 31st Annual Screen Actors Guild Awards, hosted by Kristen Bell, directed by Sandra Restrepo and Michael Dempsey, aired February 23, 2025, https://www.netflix.com/title/81745785.

CHAPTER 2:
Curiosity Compounds: Conversation and Exploration

18 *The Harvard Study of Adult Development:* Liz Mineo, "Good Genes Are Nice, but Joy Is Better," *Harvard Gazette*, April 11, 2017, https://news.harvard.edu/gazette/story/2017/04/over-nearly-80-years-harvard-study-has-been-showing-how-to-live-a-healthy-and-happy-life/.

18 *happier and healthier:* Ryan Hawk, host, *The Learning Leader Show with Ryan Hawk*, episode #509, "The World's Longest Scientific Study of Happiness, with Dr. Marc Shulz," podcast, January 22, 2023, 56 minutes, 51 seconds, https://learningleader.com/marcschulz509/.

22 *They rejected it every time:* Josh Ong, "Apple Cofounder Offered First Computer Design to HP 5 Times," *AppleInsider*, December 7, 2010, https://appleinsider.com/articles/10/12/07/apple_co_founder_offered_first_computer_design_to_hp_5_times.

23 *"a little bit too out there, too ambitious":* BUILD OR DIE (@BUILD_OR_DIE), "Sam Altman's advice for young people: 'Surround yourself with people

who will make you more ambitious . . .'" X (Twitter), June 29, 2024, https://x.com/BUILD_OR_DIE/status/1807247973090205822.

24 *factors we typically obsess over:* Nicholas A. Christakis and James H. Fowler, "Social Contagion Theory: Examining Dynamic Social Networks and Human Behavior," *Statistics in Medicine* 32, no. 4 (2013): 556–577, https://pmc.ncbi.nlm.nih.gov/articles/PMC3830455/.

24 *exactly the same weight:* Nicholas A. Christakis and James H. Fowler, "The Spread of Obesity in a Large Social Network Over 32 Years," *New England Journal of Medicine* 357, no. 4 (2007): 370–379, https://www.nejm.org/doi/full/10.1056/NEJMsa066082.

24 *whether you realize it or not:* James H. Fowler and Nicholas A. Christakis, "Dynamic Spread of Happiness in a Large Social Network: Longitudinal Analysis Over 20 Years in the Framingham Heart Study," *British Medical Journal* 337 (2008): a2338, https://pubmed.ncbi.nlm.nih.gov/19056788/.

25 *During a Q&A session:* Kevin Smith, "Burn in Hell Q&A," YouTube video, 11 minutes, 42 seconds, March 12, 2012, https://www.youtube.com/watch?v=TIVWjz0lidA&t=32s.

27 *breaking our inhibitions:* Jacob Uitti, "The Jam Band Origins of the Dave Matthews Band," *American Songwriter*, July 20, 2023, https://americansongwriter.com/the-jam-band-origins-of-the-dave-matthews-band/.

CHAPTER 3:
Question Everything: Challenging Assumptions for Growth

32 *or stay quiet:* Todd D. Jick and Mary C. Gentile, "Donna Dubinsky and Apple Computer, Inc. (A)," Harvard Business School Case 486-083, February 1986 (revised September 2011), https://www.hbs.edu/faculty/Pages/item.aspx?num=15482.

32 *"on distribution being successful":* Jick and Gentile, "Donna Dubinsky."

34 *deep mathematical understanding:* Katherine Johnson, *Reaching for the Moon: The Autobiography of NASA Mathematician Katherine Johnson* (Atheneum Books for Young Readers, 2019).

35 *mathematics and French:* Margot Lee Shetterly, "Katherine Johnson Biography," NASA, November 22, 2016, https://www.nasa.gov/centers-and-facilities/langley/katherine-johnson-biography/.

35 *verified the calculations:* Margot Lee Shetterly, *Hidden Figures: The American Dream and the Untold Story of the Black Women Mathematicians Who Helped Win the Space Race* (William Morrow, 2016).

37 *Wilbur Wright later wrote*: Wilbur Wright, "Some Aeronautical Experiments," in Annual Report of the Board of Regents of the Smithsonian Institution for the Year Ended June 30, 1902 (Washington, DC: Government Printing Office, 1903), 133–48.

37 *Seattle Longitudinal Study:* K. Warner Schaie, *Developmental Influences on Adult Intelligence: The Seattle Longitudinal Study* (Oxford University Press, 2005).

38 *George Mason University:* Todd B. Kashdan, "The Curiosity and Exploration Inventory-II: Development, Factor Structure, and Psychometrics," *Journal of Research in Personality 82 (2009):* 291–305.

40 *"good questions today":* Ismar Schorsch, "Asking Questions," Jewish Theological Seminary, January 27, 1996, https://www.jtsa.edu/torah/asking-questions/.

40 *Pulitzer Prize–winning historian:* David Hackett Fischer, *Historians' Fallacies: Toward a Logic of Historical Thought* (Harper & Row, 1970).

41 *just accepting them:* Ryan Hawk, host, *The Learning Leader Show with Ryan Hawk*, episode #342, "Shane Snow—The #1 Skill of an Effective Leader (Intellectual Humility)," podcast, Insight Global, December 8, 2019, 1 hour, 7 minutes, https://learningleader.com/episode/342-shane-snow-the-1-skill-of-an-effective-leader-intellectual-humility/.

44 *noticed this pattern:* Gokul Rajaram, "Perpetual dissatisfaction. I've now closely . . ." LinkedIn, November 14, 2024, https://www.linkedin.com/posts/gokulrajaram1_perpetual-dissatisfaction-ive-now-closely-activity-7260828359813681154-nEHR/.

CHAPTER 4:
The Hard Way: What Everyone Gets Wrong About Strength

57 *One of my favorite books:* Anne Lamott, *Bird by Bird: Some Instructions on Writing and Life* (Anchor Books, 1994).

58 "keep going up": Ryan Hawk, host, *The Learning Leader Show with Ryan Hawk*, episode #628, "How to Create Raving Fans, with Anthony Consigli," Insight Global, March 29, 2025, podcast, 56 minutes, 49 seconds, https://learningleader.com/anthonyconsigli/.

60 *"intention and obstacle":* Cal Fussman, "Aaron Sorkin: What I've Learned," *Esquire*, December 14, 2010, https://www.esquire.com/entertainment/interviews/a9103/aaron-sorkin-interview-0111/.

65 *in the 1990s:* Timothy D. Noakes, "Fatigue Is a Brain-Derived Emotion that Regulates the Exercise Behavior to Ensure the Protection of Whole-Body Homeostasis," *Frontiers in Physiology* 3 (2012): 82.

66 *when it matters:* Cameron Haines, host, *Keep Hammering Collective,* episode #301, "KCH031 – Katie Knight Podcast," July 31, 2023, audio, 46 minutes, 19 seconds, https://cameronhanes.com/blogs/podcasts/khc031-katie-knight-podcast.

69 *we'll surprise ourselves:* Ryan Hawk, host, *The Learning Leader Show with Ryan Hawk*, episode #622, "Embracing Uncertainty & The Explorer's Gene with Alex

Hutchinson," Insight Global, February 15, 2025, podcast, 59 minutes, 20 seconds, https://learningleader.com/alexhutchinson622/.

70 *"Need for Achievement":* D. C. McClelland, *The Achieving Society* (Van Nostrand Co., 1961).

71 *But newer research:* Hyunju Chung and Seungjoon Park, "Ghrelin regulates cell cycle-related gene expression in cultured hippocampal neural stem cells," *Journal of Endocrinology* 230, no. 2 (2016): 239–50, https://pubmed.ncbi.nlm.nih.gov/27325242/.

73 *he famously said*: Honda Motor Europe, "Honda Origins, History and Values in Animated Manga Comic Format," press release, April 9, 2020, https://hondanews.eu/eu/fi/cars/media/pressreleases/203177/honda-origins-history-and-values-in-animated-manga-comic-format.

77 *asked the graduates*: Roger Federer, "2024 Commencement Address," speech, Dartmouth College, Hanover, NH, June 9, 2024, video, 25 minutes, 19 seconds, https://www.youtube.com/watch?v=pqWUuYTcG-o.

CHAPTER 5:
The Long Game: Daily Inputs, Extraordinary Outputs

85 "no matter what"*:* Ryan Hawk, host, *The Learning Leader Show with Ryan Hawk*, episode #581, "Set Ambitious Goals, with Paul Rabil," Insight Global, May 5, 2024,

podcast, 50 minutes, 47 seconds, https://learningleader.com/paulrabil581/.

89 *"need to be done":* Ryan Hawk, host, *The Learning Leader Show with Ryan Hawk*, episode #306, "Brian Koppelman: Follow Your Curiosity and Obsessions with Great Rigor," April 14, 2019, podcast, 1 hour, 10 minutes, https://learningleader.com/koppelmanhawk/.

91 *effort in maintaining them:* Daniel J. Connolly, Samantha Horn, and George Loewenstein, "Inaccurate Beliefs about Skill Decay," November 9, 2025, https://ssrn.com/abstract=4916412.

92 *adopting new behaviors:* Angela L. Duckworth, Katherine L. Milkman, and David Laibson, "Beyond Willpower: Strategies for Reducing Failures of Self-Control," *Psychological Science in the Public Interest* 19, no. 3 (December 2018): 102–129, https://doi.org/10.1177/1529100618821893.

94 *"a Cinderella story":* Joe Coscarelli, "Maggie Rogers Went Viral. Then She Had to Become Herself Again," *New York Times*, January 17, 2019, https://www.nytimes.com/2019/01/17/arts/music/maggie-rogers-heard-it-in-a-past-life.html.

97 *"practice your craft":* "Philip Seymour Hoffman quote: If you get a chance to act in a room . . . ," AZQuotes, accessed July 6, 2025, https://www.azquotes.com/quote/1418353.

CHAPTER 6:
Writing and Selling: The "Art" in Articulation

111 *onto the page:* Henrik Karlsson, "When Writing, Look at What You Are Trying to Describe More than at Your Words," *Escaping Flatland*, May 22, 2025, https://www.henrikkarlsson.xyz/p/write-about-the-concrete.

113 *through complex problems:* Maryanne Wolf, *Reader, Come Home: The Reading Brain in a Digital World* (Harper, 2018).

115 *"reason to write":* Joan Didion, "Why I Write," *New York Times Book Review*, 1976.

119 *"someone has to sell":* Michael Liu, host, *View from the Top Interview*, "View From The Top with Ken Griffin, Founder and CEO of Citadel," Stanford Graduate School of Business, April 30, 2025, YouTube video, 41 minutes, 35 seconds, https://www.youtube.com/watch?v=GuF14oKon8A.

120 *"after that easier":* Ryan Hawk, host, *The Learning Leader Show with Ryan Hawk*, episode #635, "Building Celtic Pride, with Rich Gotham," Insight Global, May 15, 2025, podcast, 56 minutes, 57 seconds, https://learningleader.com/richgotham/.

121 *"Move into my house":* Howard Stern, host, *The Howard Stern Show*, "VIDEO: Maroon 5's Adam Levine and James Valentine Talk 'The Voice,' the Influence

of Grunge, and the Massive Success of 'Moves Like Jagger'," HowardStern.com, April 10, 2025, https://www.howardstern.com/show/2025/04/10/video-maroon-5s-adam-levine-and-james-valentine-talk-the-voice-the-influence-of-grunge-and-the-massive-success-of-moves-like-jagger/.

CHAPTER 7:
Trust Your Wings: Leading Without Permission

133 "You are the traffic": Eric Skelton, "Donald Glover Opens Up About His New Career Chapter, Cows, and Artificial Intelligence," *Complex*, October 16, 2024, https://www.complex.com/music/a/eric-skelton/donald-glover-interview-quiet-comfort.

134 *NPR in 2020:* Rachel Martin, host, "Chef Jose Andres Martin (World Central Kitchen) & Rachel Martin (NPR)," Skoll Foundation, YouTube video, 15 minutes, 49 seconds, April 13, 2021, https://www.youtube.com/watch?v=ctkzijxYAmE&t=285s.

134 *change and protecting nature:* Yvon Chouinard, "Earth Is Now Our Only Shareholder," Patagonia, September 14, 2022, https://www.patagonia.com/ownership/.

135 *2011 TED Talk:* Bjarke Ingels, "Hedonistic Sustainability," TEDxEast, May 2011, video, 15 minutes, 44 seconds, https://www.ted.com/talks/bjarke_ingels_hedonistic_sustainability.

137 "permission to take responsibility": Ed Catmull

and Amy Wallace, *Creativity, Inc.: Overcoming the Unseen Forces That Stand in the Way of True Inspiration* (Random House, 2014).

139 *"commit to that path":* Jeremy Stern, "American Vulcan," *Tablet*, August 14, 2024, https://www.tabletmag.com/feature/american-vulcan-palmer-luckey-anduril.

149 "we get started"*:* Ben Gilbert and David Rosenthal, *Acquired*, 2025 season, episode 1, "The Steve Ballmer Interview," J.P. Morgan Payments, January 2025, podcast, 2 hours, 59 minutes, https://www.acquired.fm/episodes/the-steve-ballmer-interview.

CHAPTER 8:
Gaining Perspective: Reflection and Intention

153 *from Insight Global:* Ryan Hawk, host, *The Learning Leader Show with Ryan Hawk*, episode #631, "Making Strategic Bets, Sam Kaufman and Bert Bean," podcast, Insight Global, April 19, 2025, 1 hour, 13 minutes, https://learningleader.com/bertsam/.

155 *information every day:* Martin Hilbert and Priscila López, "The World's Technological Capacity to Store, Communicate, and Compute Information," *Science* 332, no. 6025 (2011): 60–65. https://doi.org/10.1126/science.1200970.

157 *check less often:* Koen Inghelbrecht and Mariachiara Tedde, "Overconfidence, Financial Literacy and Excessive Trading," *Journal of Economic Behavior &*

Organization 219 (March 2024): 152–195, https://doi.org/10.1016/j.jebo.2024.01.016.

161 "buy me a beer": LaTecha Harris, "Adam Sandler's Acting Professor Told Him to Quit Acting," *Variety*, November 12, 2019, https://variety.com/2019/film/news/adam-sandler-quit-acting-1203401118/#.

163 "long time dead": David Olgilvy, *Confessions of an Advertising Man* (Atheneum, 1963).

CHAPTER 9:
The Teacher's Path: Mastery Through Mentorship

183 *the Feynman technique:* James Gleick, *Genius: The Life and Science of Richard Feynman* (Pantheon Books, 1992).

184 The Intelligent Investor: Benjamin Graham, *The Intelligent Investor: A Book of Practical Counsel* (Harper & Brothers, 1949).

184 *"they rationalize":* Jade Scipioni, "Houston Cougars coach Kelvin Sampson: Great leaders embrace confrontation—if you don't, you'll 'fail at every level,'" *CNBC*, April 7, 2025, https://www.cnbc.com/2025/04/07/houston-cougars-coach-kelvin-sampson-top-lesson-leaders-should-learn.html.

186 *not an educator:* Rita Kramer, *Maria Montessori: A Biography*, 2nd edition (Addison-Wesley, 1988).

189 *"I liked that in her":* Oprah Winfrey, "Maya Angelou

Interviewed by Oprah in 2013," *O, The Oprah Magazine*, 2013, https://www.oprah.com/omagazine/maya-angelou-interviewed-by-oprah-in-2013/all.

190 *"When you get, give"*: Elisabeth Donnelly, "Maya Angelou and Oprah's Inspiring Public Friendship," Flavorwire, May 28, 2014, https://www.flavorwire.com/459582/maya-angelou-and-oprahs-inspiring-public-friendship.

KEEP GOING

198 *It's like what Muhammad Ali said:* Muhammad Ali and Richard Durham, *The Greatest: My Own Story* (Random House, 1975).

ACKNOWLEDGMENTS

204 *"What is beauty?":* Chris Ballard, "SI Vault: Jake Plummer Walked Away from NFL to Find True Happiness," *Sports Illustrated*, June 30, 2015, https://www.si.com/nfl/2015/06/30/si-vault-jake-plummer-retirement-handball-denver-broncos.

Index

Abrams, Gracie, 141–42, 144
accountability systems, 91, 107
achievement(s)
  hunger and, 70–73
  meaningful, 69–70
Acquired (podcast), 149
actions as argument, 103–4
adaptability, 15–16
adaptation, 7–8
adversity, overcoming, 60–65, 119–20
Ali, Muhammad, 198
alignment decisions, 160–61
Altman, Sam, 23
ambition, 9–10, 13, 49
Andrés, Jose, 134
Anduril, 138
Angelou, Maya, 188–91
antifragility, 132
Apple, 23, 32–33
attentional focusing, 63
attention to details, 12, 31, 41, 75–77, 110–13, 124–25
authenticity, 5
authority, 137–38
Azure, 148–49

Ballmer, Steve, 148–49
Bannister, Roger, 11
Barker, Stephanie Wernick, 145
barriers, mental, 10–12
Bean, Bert, 153–54
The Beatles, 3–4
Beauford, Carter, 27–28
Beethoven, Ludwig van, 62
being a pro, 104–6, 107
beliefs, challenging, 48–49
Belsky, Scott, 74
better is possible framework, 59–60
Bezos, Jeff, 113
Bird by Bird (Lamott), 57

Birdflight as the Basis of Aviation (Lilienthal), 36
blinkers, 157–59, 171
Boy Meets World (TV show), 6
Brandt, Andrew, xvi
breathing life into others, 180–81
Buffett, Warren, 74, 118, 184
Burn in Hell (TV program), 25

California Redwoods, 18
capability, 66–67
careers
  combining networking with great work, 141–45
  commitment advantage, 138–41
  leading without permission, 136–38
  magnetic leadership, 149–51
  managing up, 145–48
  promotions, 129–31
  security, 131–33
  working with gusto, 163–65
casualness, 101–3, 107
Caswell, Rex, 173–74, 179, 196
Catmull, Ed, 137
Central Governor Theory, 65
Chalamet, Timothée, 9–10
challenges, overcoming, 73–75
Chamberlain, Joshua, xiv
character, 28–29
choices, 159–61
Chouinard, Yvon, 134
circle of competence, 47
Citadel, 119
Clarke, Bobby, 7–8
Clear, James, xiv, 97
cognitive development, 37–38
Cole, Kat, xiv
Coleman, Ronnie, 196
Collins, Jim, 80
comedians, 111–12
comfort, 196
commitment, 84–87, 99, 107, 138–41, 152
communication, proactive, 145–48
complexity, simplifying, 42–43, 52
confidence, 59–60
connection
  creating, 19–21
  creating space for unexpected, 30–31
  curiosity and, 17–18

a happy life and, 18
interconnectedness, 18
who you surround yourself with, 22–24
word of the year, 18–21
Consigli, Anthony, 58
consistency
in actions, 103–4
being a pro, 104–6
commitment to, 85–87
greatness and, 88
in learning, 35–36
vs. quality, 98–99
removing optionality, 92–93
control, 49–50
conversations
as acts of persuasion, 123
difficult, 184–86, 192
single-thread, 20–21
conviction, 125
copying others, 3–4, 12
craft, 112–13
Cupps, Brook, 33–34, 49
curiosity
about others, 114
asking questions, 39–41
connection and, 17–18
genuine, 21–22
innovation and, 15–16
intellectual, 40
learning and, 16
mindset of, 14–15
scientific benefits of, 37–39
writing driven by, 116
Cutler, Dave, 148–49

dabbling, 79–81
daily practice, 87–91
Damon, Matt, 187
Dave Matthews Band, 28–29, 98
da Vinci, Leonardo, 75–77, 197
decision making, 160–61
defiance, 64
Didion, Joan, 115, 122
difficult situations, navigating, 147–48
discipline, 86–87, 89–91, 159
discomfort, xv, 6–7, 15–16, 82, 196
discovery, 115–17
dissatisfaction, perpetual, 43–45, 53
distractions, filtering, 157–59, 169
doers, 177–78
“Don’t Quit” (Guest), 194–95
doubt, 36
dreams, achieving, 26–27
Drucker, Peter, 183
Dubinsky, Donna, 32–34

effort
acknowledging, 9–10
casual, 101–3
reward and, 79
The Electric Company (TV show), 96
emotional health, 31
empathy, 16
engagement, 80–81
entitlement, 77–79, 82
excellence
boring appearance of, 5, 195–96
character and, 28–29
consistency and, 35–36
contagious power of, 27–28-29
in current job roles, 129–30, 151
da Vinci's pursuit of, 75–77
as a habit, 97–100
preparation for, 197–98
surrounding yourself with, 99
sustained, 198
taking ownership, 134–36
excuse-making, avoiding, 92–93, 107
"Execute my job" mantra, 42–43
expectations, 10–12, 64, 147, 184–85
explicit monitoring, 64
external security, 131–33

failures, 52, 96–97, 102
fear, 42, 49, 82
Federer, Roger, 77
Feynman, Richard, 39, 181, 183
54 percent rule, 77
fight-or-flight response, 63
Fischer, David Hackett, 40
flourishing, 18
focus, 41–43, 63, 157–59, 169
forgiveness, 162
Framingham Heart Study, 23–24
Freeman, Morgan, 95–97
friction, 60–61, 121, 125
future self, 159–61, 171

Gandhi, Mahatma, 180
generosity, 28
George Mason University, 38
ghrelin, 71
Gilbert, Ben, 149
Glaser, Nikki, 111
Glenn, John, 35
Glover, David, 133–34
goals
avoiding excuse-making, 92–93
commitment to, 84–87

cost of casualness, 101–3
daily practice, 87–91
framework for identifying right daily action, 90–91
setting, 48–51, 52
Good Will Hunting (film), 187
Gotham, Rich, 120
Graham, Benjamin, 184
Grant, Adam, 79
gratitude, 161–62
greatness
attention to details, 75–77, 82
being a pro, 104–6
consistency and, 88
seeking, 9–10
Great Plague (1665), 155, 170
Gretzky, Walter, 7
Gretzky, Wayne, 7–8
Griffin, Ken, 119
grit, 87
growth, 6–7, 196–97
Guest, Edgar Albert, 194–95
gusto, working with, 163–65

habit(s)
compounding small, 34–36
excellence as, 99–100
following through, 90–91
writing, 124, 156
Handspring, 33
Hanes, Cameron, 66
Hanin, Yuri, 166
happy life, 18
hard things
magic of, 59–60
uncertainty in, 68–70
voluntarily doing, 73–75
hard work, 77–79
The Harvard Study of Adult Development, 18
Hemingway, Ernest, 62
Hewlett-Packard (HP), 22–23
Hewson, Marillyn, 44–45
Hillary, Edmund, 73
Hoeppner, Terry, xiii, 78, 194
Hoffman, Philip Seymour, 97
Holiday, Ryan, 115
Honda, Soichiro, 72–73
honesty, 184–86
humility, 28, 41
hundred-shots-a-day mindset, 84–91, 107
hunger, 70–73
Hutchinson, Alex, 68–69

identity, 86–87
imitation, 3–4, 12

"immigrant effect," 71–73
imposter syndrome, xv
improvement, continuous, xvi
individual zones of optimal functioning, 166
influence, 123
Ingels, Bjarke, 134–35
innovation
  curiosity and, 15–16
  hunger and, 72
insecurity, 20
Insight Global, 153–54
inspiration, 9, 180–81
intellectual engagement, 37–38
The Intelligent Investor (Graham), 184
interconnectedness, 18
internal security, 131–33
investing, 157–58

Jobs, Steve, 22–23, 32–33
Johnson, Katherine, 34–36, 52, 196
Jordan, Michael, 61–62, 63
just causes, 153–56, 171

Karlsson, Henrik, 110–11
Kashdan, Todd, 38
Kaufman, Sam, 153
Knight, Katie, 65–67
Koppelman, Brian, 14, 88–89

Lamarr, Hedy, 16
Lamott, Anne, 57
Land, Edwin, 39–40
laser-focus effect, 63
Latimore, Ed, 79–80, 138
learning
  brain and, 38
  circle of competence, 47
  consistency in, 35–36
  continuous, 45–46
  curiosity and, 16
  executing, xvii
  intake system building, xvii
  from mistakes, 46–47, 52
  teaching what you know, xvii
Learning Leader Circles, 17, 145
Learning Leader Growth Summit, 79
Learning Leader mentality, 66–67
The Learning Leader Show (podcast), xiv, 4, 5, 14, 17, 69, 74, 80, 93, 139, 153
Lennon, John, 4
Levine, Adam, 120–22
LexisNexis, 4, 119–20, 174
Lilienthal, Otto, 36–37
limitations
  moving beyond perceived, 65

questioning, 13
redirecting, 8, 13
Lincoln, Abraham, 62
Lockheed Martin, 44–45
loss aversion, 121
Lövdén, Martin, 38
luck, created by consistent preparation, 94–95
Luckey, Palmer, 138–39

magnetic leadership, 149–51, 152
managing up, 145–48, 152
Maples, Mike, Jr., 5
Maroon 5, 122
Martin, George, 4
Matthews, Dave, 27–28
Max Planck Institute, 38
McCartney, Paul, 4
McChrystal, Stanley, xiv
McClelland, David, 70
McRaven, William, xiv
Melzi, Francesco, 76
mental stamina, 67–68
mentorship
action steps, 192–93
being a great mentee, 175–78
being a great mentor, 179–88
case study, 188–91
cycle, 178–79
honesty, 184–86
inspiration, 180–81
observation, 186–88
power of, 174–75
teaching methods, 181–84
Microsoft, 148–49
mistakes, 46–47, 52, 147–48, 193
Modaff, Daniel, 103
Mona Lisa (da Vinci), 75
Montessori, Maria, 186–88
Moore, LeRoi, 27–28
motivation, 181
Munger, Charlie, 45–48, 52, 197

NASA, 34–35
Nature Communications, 71
"Need for Achievement" theory, 70–71
networking, great work and, 141–45, 152
Newton, Isaac, 155, 169, 170
Noakes, Timothy, 65
no-comfort zone, 6–7
noticing, 110–13, 124–25. *See also* observation

observation, 186–88, 193. *See also* noticing
obstacles, 60–61
Oculus VR, 138
Ogilvy, David, 163, 164–65
optimization, 199

optionality, removing, 92–93, 138–41
organizations
  failures, 33–34
  just causes, 153–55
  taking responsibility in, 137–38
ownership, 134–36, 152

Palm Computing, 33
passive aggressiveness, 184–85
Patagonia, 134
patience, 41, 144
Pedretti, Carlo, 76
perceptual narrowing, 63
Perell, David, 4
performance anxiety, 64
performance tracking, 82
persistence, 145
persuasion, 117–19, 123
Peterson, Ryan, 113
Pippen, Scottie, 61
Pixar, 136–37
Premier Lacrosse League (PLL), 87–88
preparation
  consistent, 94–95, 107
  differing approaches to, 166–68
  for excellence, 197–98
  finding your personal method of, 168–70
  variations in, 167–68
price of becoming, xvi–xvii, 67, 197, 199–200
process
  commitment to, 84–87
  daily practice, 87–91
  outcomes and, 49–50
professional antifragility, 132
professionalism, 104–6, 107
progress tracking, 107
promotions, 129–31
purpose, 9, 153–56

questions
  compounding nature of, 39
  power of good, 39–41
  questioning everything, 35–36, 39
quitting, 83

Rabi, Isidor, 40
Rabil, Paul, 49, 84–88, 99–100, 196
racehorses, 157
Rajaram, Gokul, 44
Raphael, 76
reading, 45–46, 52, 113, 156
reflection, 155–56, 169, 171
rejection, 114, 125, 161–62
relationships
  combining networking with great work, 141–45

a happy life and, 18
importance of who you surround yourself with, 22–24
inner circle audits, 31
internal security in, 132–33
magnetic, 149–51
managing up, 145–48
mentor-mentee, 175–78, 179–88, 192–93
resentment, 162
resilience, 60, 64, 68, 86
responsibility, taking, 136–38, 152
Rivas, Lee, 178
Robbins, Tony, xiv
Roethlisberger, Ben, 78
Rogers, Maggie, 94–95, 197
Rosenthal, David, 149

safety, illusion of, 26–27
sales, 114, 118, 119–20
Sampson, Kelvin, 184, 186
Sandler, Adam, 161–62
scarcity, 61
Schaie, K. Warner, 38
Schulz, Marc, 18
The Score That Matters (Hawk and Cupps), 49
Seaman, Tony, 85, 92
Seattle Longitudinal Study, 37–38
security, 131–33
self-awareness, 168–69
self-belief, 10–12
self-efficacy, 59–60, 74–75, 87
self-mastery, 172
selling, 119–23, 125
silence, 33–34
simplification, 41–43, 52
Sinek, Simon, 153
skill development, 130, 152
Smith, Donald, 25–26
Smith, J.W., 103
Smith, Kevin, 25–26
Snow, Shane, 41
solitude, 171–72
Sorkin, Aaron, 60–61
Space Race, 34–36
speaking up, 33–34
standards, 108, 184–85
Stern, Howard, 121
Stokes, Geron, 185
storytelling, 117–19
strategic intervention, 92–93
Strug, Kerry, 62
Stulberg, Brad, 18
success
compounding career capital, 96
consistent preparation, 94–95
hunger for, 71–73
perpetual dissatisfaction and, 43–44

success (*continued*)
starting small, 95–97
uncertainty and, 69
surplus-value employees, 130, 152
Susman, Galyn, 136–37
Sutcliffe, Stuart, 4
Swift, Taylor, 141–42, 144
sympathetic nervous system, 63

taking responsibility, 137–38, 152
taking the next step, 57–59, 81–82
teaching others, 181–84, 192
teamwork, 28
Toyota, 182
traffic analogy, 133–34, 135
translators, 109, 123, 126
trust, 144, 147, 179–80

uncertainty, 40–41, 68–69, 145, 199
unified teams, 33–34
urgency, sense of, 97–100

Valentine, James, 120–22
Vasari, Giorgio, 75
voice, finding your own, 5
vulnerability, 140, 144

weaknesses, redirecting, 8, 13
well-being, relationships and, 24
Williams, Pharrell, 94
Williams, Robin, 186–87
Williams, Serena, 62
Willis, Sherry L., 38
Winfrey, Oprah, 188–91
Wolf, Maryanne, 113
Woods, Tiger, 62
word of the year, 18–22
World Central Kitchen, 134
Wozniak, Steve, 22–23
Wright, Milton, 36
Wright, Orville, 36–37
Wright, Wilbur, 36–37
writing
art of selling through story, 117–19
discipline of noticing, 110–13, 124–25
habit of, 124, 156
power of discovery, 115–17
similarity to sales, 115, 123
thinking and, 114, 125

Young, Cliff, 11

About the Author

RYAN HAWK is the host of *The Learning Leader Show*, which is regularly ranked among the top business podcasts in the world, with millions of listeners annually. He is a *USA Today* bestselling author of *The Score That Matters* (with Brook Cupps) and has also written *Welcome to Management* and *The Pursuit of Excellence*. Ryan has given hundreds of keynote speeches around the world on leadership, culture, and personal excellence. And alongside the Learning Leader team of coaches, Ryan works with leadership teams at some of the most impactful companies in the world. He is also a part-time caddie (one week a year), a PA announcer (high school volleyball), and the coach of his daughter's flag football team. He lives in Dayton, Ohio, with his wife and daughters.